AN ANSWER KEY TO

A Primer of Ecclesiastical Latin

AN ANSWER KEY TO

A Primer of Ecclesiastical Latin

A Supplement to the Text by John F. Collins

Prepared by
John R. Dunlap

The Catholic University of America Press
Washington, D.C.

The paper used in this publication meets the minimum requirements of American
National Standards for Information Science—Permanence of Paper for Printed Library
Materials, ANSI Z39.48-1984.
∞

LIBRARY OF CONGRESS CATALOGING-IN-PUBLICATION DATA
    Dunlap, John, R., 1945–
        An answer key to A primer of ecclesiastical Latin : a supplement to the text
    by John F. Collins / prepared by John R. Dunlap.
            p. cm.
        Includes bibliographical references and index.
        ISBN-13: 978-0-8132-1469-6 (pbk. : alk. paper)
        ISBN-10:   0-8132-1469-6 (pbk. : alk. paper)
            1. Collins, John F., 1937–2002. Primer of ecclesiastical Latin.   2. Latin language—
    Church Latin—Grammar.   3. Liturgical language—Latin.   4. Latin language,
    Medieval and modern—Grammar.   5. Latin language, Postclassical—Grammar.
    6. Bible—Language, style.   7. Catholic Church—Liturgy.   I. Title.
        PA2823.C55 1985 Suppl.
        478—dc22   2006009566

Contents

Preface

This answer key comes in response to numerous requests over the years since the publication of John F. Collins's *Primer of Ecclesiastical Latin* in 1985. Collins himself—who died in 2002 before the issue of an answer key to his text had been resolved—envisioned his text for self-teaching as well as conventional classroom use. In addition to greater flexibility for teachers, then, the key is intended also to make the popular text more accessible to autodidacts, homeschooling families, parish seminars, and the like.

The answer key covers the regular drills, exercises, and, eventually, short readings that occur in each of the 35 units of the text. The translations of exercise sentences, especially as they become more complex, are intended to be serviceable rather than exhaustive. Intermittently, however, alternative translations are provided, in most cases for obvious reasons. The most common reason is to give a more idiomatic English rendering of a Latin expression the sense of which may not be clear with a literal translation. Such alternatives are indicated with a slash mark (/) followed by the more idiomatic English expression.

In the course of preparing this key, two issues emerged of sufficient importance to warrant some preliminary attention in the key. The first is the issue of vocabulary glosses, five of which are not expansive enough in the text's vocabulary lists to handle particular sentences in which the Latin words occur. The second is the issue of simple printing errors, which were discovered in a few units of the text. These two issues are outlined below for convenient reference.

A. Addenda

1. Unit 10, p. 85: **solvo** needs "abolish" to accommodate Exercise #3, p. 150.

2. Unit 13, p. 106: **subdo** needs "add," "supply" to accommodate Exercise #15, p. 117.

3. Unit 14, p. 114: **homo** needs "man" to accommodate the normal translation of such scriptural terms as **Filius hominis**, "Son of Man."

4. Unit 22, p. 189: **peto** needs "seek" to reveal the logic behind the idiom **peto a** [noun] **ut**.

5. Unit 33, pp. 295–96: **confero** needs "ponder" to accommodate Exercise #42, p. 300.

B. Errata

1. Unit 22, p. 187: "diaconem" should be **diaconum**.

2. Unit 22, p. 193, Reading 2, ll 3–4: flawed punctuation; change to **factum est nihil, quod factum est; in ipso** . . . (comma after **nihil**; semicolon between **est** and **in**)

3. Unit 28, p. 250, Exercise I, #19: the reference should be to Psalm li, 4 (not 6).

4. Unit 29, p. 260, Exercise I, #28: **praeterquam** is incorrectly glossed for the context; should be "contrary to" (cf. general vocabulary, p. 430).

5. Unit 30, p. 271, Exercise I, #35: **nos** should be **vos**, according to the Nova Vulgata; but the sentence is translated as-is in the key.

6. Unit 33, p. 301: the reference should be to Psalm li, 7, 1 (not 9, 3).

Apart from the addenda and errata outlined above, a few issues of translation are noted and explained as they emerge in the key. These include a consistent translation of the ablative absolute when the form occurs without a larger context, the idiomatic translation of future perfects in conditional clauses, and the normal translation of the historical present.

I am greatly obliged to several people for their encouragement and help. Particular thanks are owed to the fathers and brothers of the Carmelite Monastery in San Jose, California—students of mine who first suggested to me the need for a study aid to accompany our Collins text; to my department chairman, Bill Greenwalt, who lobbied for my sabbatical time; and especially to David J. McGonagle, director of the CUA Press, whose patience and guidance were, with respect to the whole project, **sine qua non**.

JOHN R. DUNLAP
Department of Classics
Santa Clara University
December 2005

AN ANSWER KEY TO
A Primer of Ecclesiastical Latin

Unit 1

Drills

I. PRONUNCIATION EXERCISE

Remember that the macrons (superscribed bars to indicate long vowels: quī, nōmen) are pronunciation aids, not part of the spelling. They do not appear in ordinary Latin texts (see, for example, "Further Readings," pp. 328ff.). As you acquire new vocabulary and do the exercises, you should use the macrons as an aid to pronunciation, and to the recognition of some case endings, but you should not feel obliged to memorize the placement of macrons.

II.

(Note: In the following drills, the English translations reflect a few dramatic differences between Latin and English, differences which you will soon grow accustomed to. First, Latin has no definite or indefinite article equivalent to English *the* or *a(n)*. When translating Latin nouns into English, you will often need to supply an article appropriate to the context and to English idiom. Second, three of Latin's five principal noun cases—genitive, dative, and ablative—require prepositional phrases to be translated into English. The ablative case in particular is extremely flexible, admitting a broad range of possible phrases to fit different contexts; in Latin, nouns appearing in the ablative case may come with or without Latin prepositions, but they will always need English prepositions in translation. The set of prepositions attached to the translations of ablative forms below is illustrative, not exhaustive. Cf. Collins's remarks on the ablative, p. 6.)

    a. hōrae: genitive singular ("of an/the hour")
        hōrae: dative singular ("for/to an/the hour")
        hōrae: nominative plural ("[the] hours")

    b. terram: accusative singular ("[the] land")

    c. pāpā: ablative singular ("from/with/by the pope")

    d. ecclēsiīs: dative plural ("for/to [the] churches")
        ecclēsiīs: ablative plural ("from/with/in/by [the] churches")

    e. vītārum: genitive plural ("of [the] lives")

    f. aquās: accusative plural ("[the] waters")

    g. glōria: nominative singular ("[the] glory")

    h. grātiā: ablative singular ("from/with/in/by [the] grace")

    i. missīs: dative plural ("for/to [the] Masses")
       missīs: ablative plural ("from/with/in/by [the] Masses")

    j. culpae: genitive singular ("of a/the fault")
       culpae: dative singular ("for/to a/the fault")
       culpae: nominative plural ("[the] faults")

    k. cēnae: genitive singular ("of a/the dinner")
       cēnae: dative singular ("for/to a/the dinner")
       cēnae: nominative plural ("[the] dinners")

    l. doctrīnam: accusative singular ("a/the doctrine")

    m. famīliīs: dative plural ("for/to [the] families")
        famīliīs: ablative plural ("from/with/in/by [the] families")

    n. nātūrā: ablative singular ("from/with/in/by nature")

    o. terra: nominative singular ("a/the land")

III.   a. sine pāpā ("without a/the pope")
         sine pāpīs ("without [the] popes")

b. ad glōriam ("toward/for [the purpose of] glory")
    ad glōriās ("toward/for [the purpose of] glories")

c. ā missā ("from a/the Mass")
    ā missīs ("from [the] Masses")

d. dē culpā ("from/about a/the fault")
    dē culpīs ("from/about [the] faults")

e. ad ecclēsiam "toward/for [the purpose of] a/the church")
    ad ecclēsiās ("toward/for [the purpose of] [the] churches")

Exercises

(Note: In the following translations, the selection of articles is illustrative. For example, cōram famīliā might be rendered "in the presence of the family," or "in the presence of a family," or even "in the presence of family." When you translate Latin into English, you will need context to make decisions about the choice of articles.)

I.   1. in the presence of the family

      2. toward/for [the purpose of] Mass

      3. from Mass

      4. with the pope

      5. in front of/on behalf of the church

      6. from the church

      7. toward/for [the purpose of] glory

      8. toward/for [the purpose of] the glory of the pope; toward/for [the purpose of] the glory of the pope [Notice that Latin word order is more flexible than that of English; in Latin, a highly inflected language, the grammatical sense comes more from the endings of the words than from their location in a phrase or clause. Cf. Collins's discussion of word order on p. 40.]

      9. from/concerning life; from/concerning the life of the family

      10. from/with/in/by nature; in nature

11. out of/from the lands

12. in the lands of the churches

13. into the lands

14. without family and church

15. both life and water

16. life and water

17. over the land; about the land

18. with glory

19. without fault

20. before/on behalf of the teachings of the church

II. 1. prō famīliā pāpae

2. cōram pāpā

3. sine vītā

4. ad hōram

5. ad/in glōriam ecclēsiae

Unit 2

Drills

I.   a.   agrī: genitive singular ("of a/the field")
                agrī: nominative plural ("[the] fields/country")

         b.   agnōrum: genitive plural ("of [the] lambs")

         c.   angelō: dative singular ("for/to an/the angel")
                angelō: ablative singular ("from/with/in/by an/the angel)

         d.   archangelīs: dative plural ("for/to [the] archangels")
                archangelīs: ablative plural ("from/with/in/by [the] archangels")

         e.   apostolōs: accusative plural ("[the] apostles")

         f.   Christī: genitive singular ("of Christ")

         g.   Deō: dative singular ("for/to God")
                Deō: ablative singular ("from/with/in/by God")

         h.   discipulīs: dative plural ("for/to [the] disciples")
                discipulīs: ablative plural ("from/with/in/by [the] disciples")

         i.   dominum: accusative singular ("a/the master")

         j.   episcopī: genitive singular ("of a/the bishop")
                episcopī: nominative plural ("[the] bishops")

         k.   filius: nominative singular ("a/the son")

         l.   minister: nominative singular ("a/the minister")

    m. Petrō: dative singular ("for/to Peter")
       Petrō: ablative singular ("from/with/in/by Peter")

    n. puerum: accusative singular ("a/the boy")

    o. psalmōrum: genitive plural ("of [the] psalms")

II.   a. *Agrī sunt* in Jūdaeā. The fields are in Judea.
       Ager est in Jūdaeā. A/the field is in Judea.

    b. *Ancillae sumus.* We are [the] maids.
       Ancilla sum. I am a/the maid.

    c. *Apostolus est* in Jūdaeā. An/the apostle is in Judea.
       Apostolī sunt in Jūdaeā. The apostles are in Judea.

    d. *Discipulī estis.* You are [the] disciples.
       Discipulus es. You are a/the disciple.

    e. *Minister* nōn *est* in Jūdaeā. A/the minister is not in Judea.
       Ministrī nōn *sunt* in Jūdaeā. The ministers are not in Judea.

Exercises

I.   1. Water is on earth. / There is water on earth.

    2. The church is on earth. / There is a church on earth.

    3. The disciples of Christ are in Judea. / There are disciples of Christ in Judea.

    4. For he is the Lamb of God.

    5. Both power and justice are on earth. / There are both power and justice on earth.

    6. Peter is not in the fields.

    7. Today the boys are not in church.

    8. Mary is the servant of the Lord.

    9. The angels and archangels are not from earth.

    10. We are the ministers of God.

11. in the psalms; across the fields; from the apostles; in the presence of the servant; from the boys; toward the son; with the bishop; without the people of God; in glory and power.

II.   1. Puer nōn est in agrō.

2. Nam populus Deī sumus.

3. Petrus est pāpa.

4. Sunt et apostolī et discipulī.

5. Episcopus est minister populī.

6. Pāpa est Servus Servōrum.

Unit 3

Drills

I. a. caelum: nominative singular ("heaven")
        caelum: accusative singular ("heaven")

    b. canticō: dative singular ("for/to a/the song")
        canticō: ablative singular ("from/with/in/by a/the song")

    c. dōna: nominative plural ("[the] gifts")
        dōna: accusative plural ("[the] gifts")

    d. Evangeliīs: dative plural ("for/to [the] Gospels")
        Evangeliīs: ablative plural ("from/with/in/by [the] Gospels")

    e. fēstī: genitive singular ("of a/the feast")

    f. gaudiōrum: genitive plural ("of [the] joys")

    g. mystērium: nominative singular ("a/the mystery")
        mystērium: accusative singular ("a/the mystery")

    h. odia: nominative plural ("[the] hatreds")
        odia: accusative plural ("[the] hatreds")

    i. caelī: genitive singular ("of heaven")

    j. sabbatīs: dative plural ("for/to [the] Sabbaths")
        sabbatīs: ablative plural ("from/with/in/by [the] Sabbaths")

    k. praecepta: nominative plural ("[the] lessons")
        praecepta: accusative plural ("[the] lessons")

l. sacrificiō: dative singular ("for/to a/the sacrifice")
    sacrificiō: ablative singular ("from/with/in/by a/the sacrifice")

m. testāmentī: genitive singular ("of a/the testament")

n. vīnōrum: genitive plural ("of [the] wines")

o. vitiīs: dative plural ("for/to [the] faults")
    vitiīs: ablative plural ("from/with/in/by [the] faults")

II.   a. *Librī erant* hīc. The books were here.
          Liber erat hīc. A/the book was here.

      b. In Jūdaeā *apostolus erat.* An/the apostle was in Judea.
          In Jūdaeā *apostolī erant.* The apostles were in Judea.

      c. *Servī* Dominī *erimus.* We will be servants of the Lord.
          Servus Dominī *ero.* I will be a servant of the Lord.

      d. *Ministrī eritis.* You will be [the] ministers.
          Minister eris. You will be a/the minister.

      e. *Liber est* apostolō. The apostle has a book.
          Librī sunt apostolō. The apostle has books.

Exercises

I.   1. Christ has power and glory.

      2. It is the mystery of water and of wine.

      3. The kingdom of God will be forever.

      4. The apostles were ministers of Christ.

      5. There will be joy in heaven.

      6. The Sabbath is the feast of the Lord.

      7. Both hymns and songs are in the book.

      8. Hatred and sin are in the world.

      9. The Gospel is a gift of God to the people.

      10. Mary is the Queen of Heaven.

11. Here is the word of God.

12. The man will have a reward there.

13. The choir of angels has joy.

14. God and the people have a covenant.

15. The boys will be disciples of the Lord.

16. The sons of the man were ministers of the word.

17. The sacrifice of Christ was a gift of God.

18. Christ was and is and will be Lord of the universe.

19. Hatred of sin is not a vice.

20. The pope has the grace of God.

21. We are the people of justice on earth.

II. 1. Pāpa est Ecclēsiae.

2. Vīta et gaudium sunt et in caelō et in terrā.

3. In vītā servī Dominī sumus.

4. Episcopus nōn erat populō.

5. Nam rēgnum caelī est hīc.

Unit 4

Drills

I.   a.   bonā aquā: "from/with/in/by [the] good water"
            bonīs aquīs: "from/with/in/by [the] good waters"

    b.   antīquīs ministrīs: "for/to [the] old ministers" (dat. pl.)
            antīquō ministrō: "for/to an/the old minister (dat. sg.)

            antīquīs ministrīs: "from/with/in/by [the]old ministers" (abl. pl.)
            antīquō ministrō: "from/with/in/by an/the old minister (abl. sg.)

    c.   multus angelus: "many an angel"
            multī angelī: "many angels"

    d.   pāpae novō: "for/to a/the new pope"
            pāpīs novīs: "for/to [the] new popes"

    e.   vērum Deum: "[the] true God"
            vērōs deōs: "[the] true gods"

    f.   tuae culpae: "of your fault" (gen. sg.)
            tuārum culpārum: "of your faults"

            tuae culpae: "for/to your fault" (dat. sg.)
            tuīs culpīs: "for/to your faults"

            tuae culpae: "your faults" (nom. pl.)
            tua culpa: "your fault"

g. apostolō beatō: "for/to a/the blessed apostle" (dat. sg.)
    apostolīs beatīs: "for/to [the] blessed apostles"

    apostolō beatō: "from/with/in/by a/the blessed apostle (abl. sg.)
    apostolīs beatīs: "from/with/in/by [the] blessed apostles"

h. magna glōria: "great glory"
    magnae glōriae: "great glories"

i. discipulī sacrī: "of a/the holy disciple" (gen. sg.)
    discipulōrum sacrōrum: "of [the] holy disciples"

    discipulī sacrī: "[the] holy disciples" (nom. pl.)
    discipulus sacer: "a/the holy disciple"

j. aeterna testāmenta "[the] eternal covenants"
    aeternum testāmentum: "an/the eternal covenant"

k. impiārum vītārum: "of [the] wicked lives"
    impiae vītae: "of a/the wicked life"

l. sacrae rēgīnae: "of a/the holy queen" (gen. sg.)
    sacrārum rēgīnārum: "of [the] holy queens"

    sacrae rēgīnae: "for/to [the] holy queen" (dat. sg.)
    sacrīs rēgīnīs: "for/to [the] holy queens"

    sacrae rēgīnae: "[the] holy queens" (nom. pl.)
    sacra rēgīna: "a/the holy queen"

Exercises

I.   1. Where are (there) many disciples?

      2. My church is your church; my church (is) your church; mine (is) your church.

      3. Blessed (are) the servants of the Lord.

      4. The Lord God of hosts is holy.

      5. There is much joy for the holy people of God.

      6. The way of the world is both good and bad; the ways of the world are good and bad.

7. Great is the number of (the) angels.

8. The new covenant is the word of God.

9. Christ is Lord of both the living and the dead.

10. The mysteries of God are eternal.

11. Clear on earth and in heaven (is) the word of God.

12. To God [there] is a holy son forever. / God has a holy son forever.

13. The spirit of the man is blessed and good.

14. Christ was the teacher of Peter and of the apostles.

15. There will be gold for the boy in the upper room.

16. The sword of Peter was wicked.

17. Here is our sacrament.

18. Our nature (is) a gift of God.

19. The supper of the Lord is for our people.

20. Many in Judea were disciples of Christ.

21. From/about the new covenant; in great heaven(s); without our many faults; in the presence of God.

22. The apostle does not have gold. [Acts iii, 6, adapted]

23. My teaching is not mine. [Jn. vii,16]

24. A disciple is not above (his) teacher nor a servant above (his) master. [Mt. x, 24]

II.   1. Vīvus Deus est sacer.

2. Vīvī erunt mortuī, mortuī vīvī.

3. Antīquī nostrī erant servī Dominī.

4. Verbum tuum est praeceptum nostrum.

5. Rēgnum Deī est in aeternum.

Unit 5

Drills

I. a. ambulāmus: "we walk" / "we are walking"
        ambulō: "I walk" / "I am walking"

    b. cantās: "you (sg.) sing" / "you (sg.) are singing"
        cantātis: "you (pl.) sing" / "you (pl.) are singing"

    c. dōnant: "they give" / "they are giving"
        dōnat: "he/she/it gives" / "he/she/it is giving"

    d. laudat: "he/she/it praises" / "he/she/it is praising"
        laudant: "they praise" / "they are praising"

    e. adōrātis: "you (pl.) worship" / "you (pl.) are worshiping"
        adōrās: "you (sg.) worship" / "you (sg.) are worshiping"

    f. rēgnat: "he/she/it rules" / "he/she/it is ruling"
        rēgnant: "they rule" / "they are ruling"

    g. cōnservās: "you (sg.) keep" / "you (sg.) are keeping"
        cōnservātis: "you (pl.) keep" / "you (pl.) are keeping"

    h. invocāmus: "we call upon" / "we are calling upon"
        invocō: "I call upon" / "I am calling upon"

    i. operant: "they work" / "they are working"
        operat: "he/she/it works" / "he/she/it is working"

    j. collaudātis: "you (pl.) praise together" / "you (pl.) are praising together"
        collaudās: "you (sg.) praise together" / "you (sg.) are praising together"

II.   a. The disciples give/are giving an example to the people.

      b. The man gives/is giving a book to the boy.

      c. Peter gives/is giving a reward to the servant.

      d. We give/are giving gold to the queen.

      e. You (pl.) give/are giving a gift to the teacher.

Exercises

I.   1. Holy, Holy, Holy Lord God of hosts.

      2. Christ calls / is calling the apostles.

      3. In the Mass the people of God praise the Lord.

      4. We do not give / are not giving gifts to wicked men.

      5. We walk / are walking in the way of the Lord.

      6. Rightly we praise / are praising the Lord together; for he is holy and good.

      7. The bishop also calls upon / is calling upon God on behalf of the church.

      8. The Lord always frees / is freeing (his) people from evil.

      9. Christ always reigns / is always reigning in our souls.

     10. The disciples work / are working with the apostles.

     11. We sing / are singing a psalm in the presence of the Lord.

     12. We pray / are praying for the life of the world.

     13. The minister calls / is calling the people to the supper of the Lord.

14. The servant praises / is praising the star in heaven.

15. We the just never observe / are never observing the words of the wicked.

16. For rightly you (sg.) praise / are praising exceedingly Christ, the son of God.

17. The shining example of Mary is for the people. / The people have . . .

18. Now the blest make holy / are making holy the Sabbath.

19. Peter summons / is summoning the boys from the fields.

20. To the church we give / are giving and for the people we work / are working.

21. Are you the Christ the son of the Blest One? [Mk. xiv, 61]

II.   1. Ad Deum orāmus.

2. Deus vītam mundō dat.

3. Virī bonī Dominum semper laudant.

4. Episcopus noster aquam et vīnum cōnsecrat.

5. Deus in caelō rēgnat, pāpa in terrā.

6. In prīncipiō erat Verbum. [Jn. i, 1]

7. Meritō populus Dominum Vītae laudat.

Unit 6

Drill𝛛

I. a. reddis: "you (sg.) give back" / "you (sg.) are giving back"
        redditis: "you (pl.) give back" / "you (pl.) are giving back"

    b. dēlētis: "you (pl.) destroy" / "you (pl.) are destroying"
        dēlēs: "you (sg.) destroy" / "you (sg.) are destroying"

    c. habēmus: "we have" / "we are having"
        habeō: "I have" / "I am having"

    d. agit: "he/she/it does" / "he/she/it is doing"
        agunt: "they do" / "they are doing"

    e. crēdō: "I believe" / "I am believing"
        crēdimus: "we believe" / "we are believing"

    f. capiunt: "they take" / "they are taking"
        capit: "he/she/it takes" / "he/she/it is taking"

    g. facis: "you (sg.) make" / "you (sg.) are making"
        facitis: "you (pl.) make" / "you (pl.) are making"

    h. audīmus: "we hear" / "we are hearing"
        audiō: "I hear" / "I am hearing"

    i. advenīs: "you (sg.) arrive" / "you (sg.) are arriving"
        advenītis: "you (pl.) arrive" / "you (pl.) are arriving"

    j. ēdūcitis: "you (pl.) lead out" / "you (pl.) are leading out"
        ēdūcis: "you (sg.) lead out" / "you (sg.) are leading out"

II.   a. Do you call the boy? / Are you calling the boy?

        b. Does he walk to (the) church? / Is he walking to (the) church?

        c. Do they sing a hymn? / Are they singing a hymn? They sing/are singing a hymn.

        d. Does he arrive at/come to Judea? / Is he arriving at/coming to Judea?

        e. Do you (pl.) keep the word of God? / Are you (pl.) keeping the word of God?

Exercises

(Note: In most instances, the verbs in the following sentences may be translated alternatively in the progressive aspect: puts to flight / is putting to flight. When you translate Latin, you need a larger context to decide which aspect to use. Review Collins on simple and progressive aspect, pp. 34–36.)

I.   1. On behalf of the Hebrews the Lord puts to flight the Egyptians.

        2. We always give thanks to God.

        3. With (his) eternal precepts the Lord warns (his) people.

        4. Mary finds (her) son in the temple.

        5. The bishop leads the people into the church.

        6. Peter arrives at the house with (his) disciples.

        7. Do we drink the wine of life with joy?

        8. Why does the apostle betray Christ to the wicked?

        9. The wicked servant deceives the boy with gold.

        10. Christ unites (his) people in glory.

        11. With (his) precepts the pope leads the church.

        12. Now the minister mixes the wine with water.

        13. The people of God come together into church and our bishop conducts Mass.

14. Either by psalm or by sacrifice together we praise the glory of the Lord.

15. Do the chosen always believe in God?

16. With great joy we Christians hear the teachings of Christ.

17. With the sacrifice of (his) Son God wipes out the sins of (his) people.

18. Without Christ we fail; for he preserves (his) people.

19. Do they still take gold from the wicked? The wicked do not affect the holy with good example.

20. The blest both hear and keep the words of the Lord.

21. Does my servant lead the boy across the field to the house?

22. In Christ we have a holy example.

23. With Christ we never do wicked things.

24. We consider God (to be) good and holy.

25. Does the minister give wine to the teacher?

26. Christ affects (his) people with joy.

27. Does the boy understand the beginning of the Gospel?

28. The maid-servant leads your son into the house.

29. They do not have wine. [Jn. ii, 3]

30. The hour comes, and it is now. [Jn. v, 25]

II.   1. Trāditne apostolus impius Chrīstum?

2. Habēmusne Chrīstiānī odium peccātī?

3. Minister noster prō populō sacrificium facit.

4. Venitne Chrīstus cum glōriā?

5. Dominō grātiās agimus, nam malōs fugat.

6. Redditne servus/famulus aurum magistrō/dominō?

Unit 7

Drills

I.   a. audīris: "you (sg.) are (being) heard"
          audīminī: "you (pl.) are (being) heard"

      b. capitur: "he/she/it is (being) taken"
          capiuntur: "they are (being) taken"

      c. jungor: "I am (being) joined"
          jungimur: "we are (being) joined"

      d. dūcuntur: "they are (being) led"
          dūcitur: "he/she/it is (being) led"

      e. monētur: "he/she/it is (being) warned"
          monentur: "they are (being) warned"

      f. dēlēminī: "you (pl.) are (being) destroyed"
          dēlēris/dēlēre: "you (sg.) are (being) destroyed"

      g. fugāmur: "we are (being) put to flight"
          fugor: "I am (being) put to flight"

      h. ēdūcere: "you (sg.) are (being) led out"
          ēdūciminī: "you (pl.) are (being) led out"

      i. trādiminī: "you (pl.) are (being) betrayed"
          trāderis/trādere: "you (sg.) are (being) betrayed"

      j. inveniuntur: "they are (being) found"
          invenītur: "he/she/it is (being) found"

k. exaudīmur: "we are (being) heard favorably"
   exaudior: "I am (being) heard favorably"

l. laudor: "I am (being) praised"
   laudāmur: "we are (being) praised"

II. a. laudat: "he/she/it praises / is praising"
        laudātur: "he/she/it is (being) praised"

     b. dōnāmur: "we are (being) given"
        dōnāmus: "we give / are giving"

     c. liberāminī: "you (pl.) are (being) freed"
        liberātis: "you (pl.) free / are freeing"

     d. servant: "they keep / are keeping"
        servantur: "they are (being) kept"

     e. vocās: "you (sg.) call / are calling"
        vocāris/vocāre: "you (sg.) are (being) called"

     f. habentur: "they are (being) had"
        habent: "they have / are having"

     g. miscētur: "he/she/it is (being) mixed"
        miscet: "he/she/it mixes / is mixing"

     h. dūcitis: "you (pl.) lead / are leading"
        dūciminī: "you (pl.) are (being) led"

     i. perdūcuntur: "they are (being) led through"
        perdūcunt: "they lead through / are leading through

     j. capiō: "I take / am taking"
        capior: "I am (being) taken"

     k. recipitur: "he/she/it is (being) taken back"
        recipit: "he/she/it takes back / is taking back

     l. invenīs: "you (sg.) find / are finding"
        invenīris/invenīre: "you (sg.) are (being) found"

Exercises

I.   1. Full are the heavens and the earth with your glory.

2. Jesus of Nazareth is called (the) Christ.

3. A reward is (being) given by the teacher to the boy.

4. Jesus heals the crowd; for many are sick.

5. Today Mass is (being) celebrated by the beloved bishop.

6. Are we worthy of the mercy of God?

7. The sick boy is (being) healed by the prayers of Peter.

8. All Judea arrives at home, and by Jesus (their) sins are (being) forgiven.

9. The minister prays well, and the first response is (being) said by the people.

10. At first Jesus heals the sick and the sad.

11. In the liturgy God is (being) praised by the people.

12. Because of the victory of Christ the apostles were full of joy; and still with joy the people always bless the Lord.

13. Do we always bless the souls of the just?

14. Together with the people the worthy deacon prays to God.

15. The apostle dear to Jesus leads Mary into the upper room.

16. Both the worthy and the unworthy are kept by God.

17. One maid-servant comes to Jesus in the house, and she is blessed.

18. With great joy the psalms are sung by the disciples.

19. Because of the Son of God our nature is freed from sin.

20. The Lord reigns in our souls; for he destroys our vices and faults.

21. By (his) family the boy Jesus is found with teachers in the temple.

22. The book is taken back by the first deacon.

23. At first the servant is led into the house; there they tell the servant to take water.

24. And you, you were with this Nazarene, Jesus. [Mk. xiv, 67]

25. I believe in one God.

26. Is the liturgy of the Word now being conducted?

II. 1. Populus bonus in ecclēsiam ā diācōnō novō indūcitur; ibi cantica Dominī cum laetitiā cantantur.

  2. Hodiē victōria aeterna Chrīstī ā populō bene celebrātur.

  3. Multa dōna ecclēsiae ā ministrō cārō accipiuntur.

  4. Meritō Dominus potentiae et jūstitiae nātūrā ūniversā laudātur.

  5. Vir nōn est maestus sed plēnus gaudiō, nam īnfirmī in Jūdaeā āb apostolīs benedictīs sānantur.

Unit 8

Drillɟ

I.
a. cantābātur: "he/she/it was being sung"
cantābat: "he/she/it was singing"

b. dabāminī: "you (pl.) were being given"
dabātis: "you (pl.) were giving"

c. laudābāre: "you (sg.) were being praised"
laudābās: "you (sg.) were praising"

d. līberābantur: "they were being freed"
līberābant: "they were freeing"

e. dēlēbar: "I was being destroyed"
dēlēbam: "I was destroying"

f. monēbāmur: "we were being warned"
monēbāmus: "we were warning"

g. agēbāre: "you (sg.) were being done"
agēbās: "you (sg.) were doing"

h. dūcēbātur: "he/she/it was being led"
dūcēbat: "he/she/it was leading"

i. perdūcēbāris: "you (sg.) were being led through"
perdūcēbās: "you (sg.) were leading through"

j. inveniēbāminī: "you (pl.) were being found"
inveniēbātis: "you (pl.) were finding"

    k. sānābātur: "he/she/it was being healed"
         sānābat: "he/she/it was healing"

    l. cōnfirmābar: "I was being strengthened"
         cōnfirmābam: "I was strengthening"

II.   a. dōnābat: "he/she/it was giving"
         dōnābant: "they were giving"

    b. laudābāminī: "you (pl.) were being praised"
         laudābāris/laudābāre: "you (sg.) were being praised"

    c. adōrābātur: "he/she/it was being worshipped"
         adōrābantur: "they were being worshipped"

    d. efficiēbantur: "they were being made / were becoming"
         efficiēbātur: "he/she/it was being made / was becoming"

    e. vocābās: "you (sg.) were calling"
         vocābātis: "you (pl.) were calling"

    f. observābāmur: "we were being watched"
         observābar: "I was being watched"

    g. miscēbāris: "you (sg.) were being mixed"
         miscēbāminī: "you (pl.) were being mixed"

    h. recipiēbantur: "they were being taken back"
         recipiēbātur: "he/she/it was being taken back"

    i. inveniēbat: "he/she/it was finding"
         inveniēbant: "they were finding"

    j. firmābās: "you (sg.) were strengthening"
         firmābātis: "you (pl.) were strengthening"

    k. sānābāminī: "you (pl.) were being healed"
         sānābāris/sānābāre: "you (sg.) were being healed"

    l. celebrābam: "I was celebrating"
         celebrābāmus: "we were celebrating"

Exercises

I.   1. The boy was being raised up (is being raised up) by the power of God.

2. God was being praised by the angelic multitude of heaven.

3. Through the power of Christ the people were being healed by the apostles.

4. The house was (being) filled with a sad silence, because the boy was dead.

5. The apostles were (being) filled with joy, because the word of the Lord was (being) fulfilled.

6. When was the boy (being) corrected by the teacher?—Not today.

7. The Hebrews were praising the glorious Lord with psalms and incense, because wonderful things were still being accomplished for the people.

8. The deacon says that the Lord hears the prayers of the contrite.

9. With contrite heart we were giving thanks to God, but the wicked (were) not.

10. All the disciples were now coming into the house after Jesus.

11. There is joy both in heavenly and in earthly things, because the Lord is good and great.

12. The boys were now finding that both hymns and songs are in the wonderful book.

13. The wicked minister was not making a pure sacrifice.

14. Our ministers say that Christ was and is and will be Lord of all nature.

15. Again we were being taught (are being taught) by the salutary teachings of Christ.

16. The apostle kept hearing that Jesus was alive, but he did not believe. [For the parenthetical **est,** see Collins, note 4, p. 69. Idiomatic English uses past *was* for both.]

17. Always you were saying that many in Judea were disciples of Christ.

18. Then the disciples were walking with Jesus through the fields.

19. Through the merits of Jesus we were being healed and were being made steadfast.

20. We are blessed, because God has a loving son forever.

21. Today the words of the ancients are fulfilled in the presence of the Jews.

22. Through a most holy sacrament we were (being) made pleasing to the Lord.

23. A great crowd was gathering at the house, because they were hearing that Jesus of Nazareth was there.

24. Then Peter was blessing the crowd, and was speaking about the mercy of our Lord Jesus Christ.

25. But the hour comes, and it is now. [Jn. iv, 23]

II. 1. Dicunt quia Petrus prīmus pāpa erat.

2. Tū quoque Deum laudābās psalmīs et canticīs.

3. Semper grātiā Deī firmābāmur.

4. Est odium peccātī sed misericordia prō contrītīs.

5. Tua verba vēra et vīva per mundum ā cūnctō populō audiuntur.

Unit 9

Drills

I.   a. ambulābis: "you (sg.) will walk"
         ambulās: "you (sg.) walk"

   b. cantābuntur: "they will be sung"
        cantantur: "they are (being) sung"

   c. dabit: "he/she/it will give"
        dat: "he/she/it gives"

   d. collaudābitis: "you (pl.) will praise exceedingly"
        collaudātis: "you (pl.) praise exceedingly"

   e. līberābimur: "we will be freed"
        līberāmur: "we are (being) freed"

   f. operābo: "I will work"
        operō: "I work"

   g. servābiminī: "you (pl.) will be kept"
        servāminī: "you (pl.) are (being) kept"

   h. vocābere: "you (sg.) will be called"
        vocāris/vocāre: "you (sg.) are (being) called"

   i. invocābimus: "we will call upon"
        invocāmus: "we call upon"

   j. fugābunt: "they will put to flight"
        fugant: "they put to flight"

    k. monēbor: "I will be warned"
         moneor: "I am warned"

    l. habēberis: "you (sg.) will be had"
         habēris/habēre: "you (sg.) are had"

II.   a. agētur: "he/she/it will be done"
         agitur: "he/she/it is (being) done"

    b. bibēmus: "we will drink"
         bibimus: "we drink"

    c. crēdent: "they will believe"
         crēdunt: "they believe"

    d. dūcet: "he/she/it will lead"
         dūcit: "he/she/it leads"

    e. capiēmur: "we will be taken"
         capimur: "we are (being) taken"

    f. faciēs: "you (sg.) will make"

         facis: "you (sg.) make"

    g. veniētis: "you (pl.) will come"
         venītis: "you (pl.) come"

    h. adveniam: "I will arrive"
         adveniō: "I arrive"

    i. regar: "I will be ruled"
         regor: "I am (being) ruled"

    j. maledīcentur: "they will be cursed"
         maledīcuntur: "they are (being) cursed"

    k. corrigēre: "you (sg.) will be corrected"
         corrigeris/corrigere: "you (sg.) are (being) corrected"

    l. ēdūcēminī: "you (pl.) will be led out"
         ēdūciminī: "you (pl.) are (being) led out"

Exercises

I.   1. But the good in spirit will be separated (were being separated) from the wicked.

2. The commandments of God will be known (are known) by your people.

3. We will always praise our Lord, because he surely rules the universe.

4. Will boys sad in spirit diligently work in the fields?

5. We believe in one holy, catholic and apostolic Church.

6. Jesus was entering in the house (lit.: under the roof) of the servant, and immediately the boy was healed.

7. Peter often was seeing Mary among the companions of the dear apostle.

8. For the sake of the people Peter will produce (produces, was producing) testimony about Jesus.

9. Your companions will be trained by the deacon in the commandments of the Lord.

10. Peter sees that it is good to be here.

11. We know that the church will always give testimony about Christ Jesus.

12. On the road of life we will always be led through (are led through, were being led through) by the footsteps of the Lord.

13. Candles will be given (were being given, are given) to the people by the deacon.

14. The supper of the Lord was satisfying (will satisfy, satisfies) the people.

15. The apostle often was producing testimony about the lamb of God.

16. The boys will help the men in the fields.

17. The joy of the disciple (is) full, because he guides the people in the power of God.

18. They saw the bright star, and immediately they praised the High God.

19. But Peter will come out of the house, and he will see your companions.

20. The mercy of God is the cause of much joy.

21. The child will be found (is being found, was being found) among the teachers.

22. Truly happy are the companions, because they are nourished and helped by the High God.

23. We saw your child in the temple; and there he was speaking wondrous things.

24. When will the Lord come again with glory?

25. For you know the grace of our Lord Jesus Christ. [II Cor. viii, 9]

II. 1. Altus Deus ā ministrō et populō laudābitur.

2. Bonum est operāre prō rēgnō.

3. Servī causā bonī Jēsūs domum intrābit et puerum sānābit.

4. In silentiō grātiās Dominō agēmus.

5. Per potentiam Jēsū (ā) malō līberābimur. [See the ablative of separation in Collins, p. 41.]

Unit 10

Drillₐ

I. sum, esse, fuī, futūrus

          fuī   fuimus

          fuistī   fuistis

          fuit   fuērunt

adōrō, adōrāre, adōrāvī, adōrātus

          adōrāvī   adōrāvimus

          adōrāvistī   adōrāvistis

          adōrāvit   adōrāvērunt

compleō, complēre, complēvī, complētus

          complēvī   complēvimus

          complēvistī   complēvistis

          complēvit   complēvērunt

regō, regere, rēxī, rēctus

          rēxī   rēximus

          rēxistī   rēxistis

          rēxit   rēxērunt

accipiō, accipere, accēpī, acceptus

accēpī	accēpimus
accēpistī	accēpistis
accēpit	accēpērunt

veniō, venīre, vēnī, ventus

vēnī	vēnimus
vēnistī	vēnistis
vēnit	vēnērunt

II. a. cantāvistis: "you (pl.) (have) sung"
cantābātis: "you (pl.) were singing"

b. laudābāmus: "we were praising"
laudāvimus: "we (have) praised"

c. vocābātis: "you (pl.) were calling"
vocāvistis: "you (pl.) (have) called"

d. habuērunt: "they (have) had"
habēbant: "they were having"

e. faciēbam: "I was making"
fēcī: "I (have) made"

f. dūxistī: "you (sg.) (have) led"
dūcēbās: "you (sg.) were leading"

g. invēnit: "he/she/it (has) found"
inveniēbat: "he/she/it was finding"

h. crēdēbās: "you (sg.) were believing"
crēdidistī: "you (sg.) (have) believed"

i. sānāvī: "I (have) healed"
sānābam: "I was healing"

j. dīcēbat: "he/she/it was saying"
dīxit: "he/she/it (has) said"

k. replēvimus: "we (have) completed"
   replēbāmus: "we were completing"

l. vidēbant: "they were seeing"
   vīdērunt: "they saw (have seen)"

Exercises

I.   1. Glory in the highest to God.

2. The minister and servants prayed: Lord, have mercy!

3. The Lord, who is good, always knew the desires of (his) people.

4. The servant, whom you know, gave both water and wine to the minister.

5. The apostles (have) handed down the words of Christ, which we hear.

6. Which disciples in Galilee knew that Jesus of Nazareth was the only begotten son of God?

7. According to your words we (have) worked and we (have) prayed constantly.

8. To which servant was the master not dear?

9. Through (his) only begotten Son God pays back the debts of our sins.

10. The Lamb of God, who takes away the sins of the world, is always praised by (his) people.

11. Today the Lord God has lifted up (his) only begotten Son above all in heaven and on earth. Alleluia.

12. Through the perpetual mercy of God the chains of sin are lifted and are broken.

13. Which disciples (have) finished their life in Galilee?

14. Afterwards Christians were (being) affected by the loss of Peter.

15. Blessed (is he) who comes to the supper of the Lord. Hosanna in the highest!

16. Suddenly the boy saw the power of the Lord. And he gave thanks to God.

17. The clergy often are aided by the service of the people.

18. The first disciple knew Peter, but the second (did) not.

19. The sick entered into the house. And they were healed by Jesus.

20. Through the space of many years the apostles of Jesus Christ were seen in Galilee. For they truly believed in Jesus.

21. Through the power of the Lord, Peter absolved the people from (their) sins.

22. Mary saw (sees) (her) son in front of the teachers.

23. The men, with whom Jesus was walking across the fields, were (his) disciples.

24. And again he entered Capharnaum. [Mk. ii, 1]

25. I know that the Messiah comes—(the one) who is called the Christ. [Jn. iv, 25]

II.   1. Quae vīta est bona et beāta?

   2. Puer quem vīdimus est nātus servī.

   3. Quī servī Dominī sunt sine culpā?

   4. Ecce Agnus Deī, quī tollit peccātum mundī. [Jn. i, 29]

   5. Discipulus quī populum adjūvit ministerium in Jūdaeā fīnīvit.

Unit 11

Drills

I. a. ambulāverat: "he/she/it had walked"
ambulāverant: "they had walked"

b. dederāmus: "we had given"
dederam: "I had given"

c. dōnāverimus: "we will have given"
dōnāverō: "I will have given"

d. laudāverint: "they will have praised"
laudāverit: "he/she/it will have praised"

e. dēlēverit: "he/she/it will have destroyed"
dēlēverint: "they will have destroyed"

f. miscuerātis: "you (pl.) had mixed"
miscuerās: "you (sg.) had mixed"

g. ēgerant: "they had done"
ēgerat: "he/she/it had done"

h. dūxerō: "I will have led"
dūxerimus: "we will have led"

i. dīxeris: "you (sg.) will have said"
dīxeritis: "you (pl.) will have said"

j. affirmāveritis: "you (pl.) will have proven"
affirmāveris: "you (sg.) will have proven"

k. adimplēverās: "you (sg.) had fulfilled"
    adimplēverātis: "you (pl.) had fulfilled"

l. rēxerit: "he/she/it will have ruled"
    rēxerint: "they will have ruled"

m. dīrēxerat: "he/she/it had directed"
    dīrēxerant: "they had directed"

n. scīverāmus: "we had known"
    scīveram: "I had known"

o. solveram: "I had set free"
    solverāmus: "we had set free"

II. a. he had finished: fīnīverat

b. we will have absolved: absolverimus

c. they had had: habuerant

d. you will have seen: vīderis

e. I had warned: monueram

f. I will have said: dīxerō

g. you (pl.) had taken: cēperātis

h. they will have healed: sānāverint

i. she had celebrated: celebrāverat

j. he will have known: scīverit

Exercises

I. 1. Because the Hebrews saw the pillar of flame, even today they observe the Passover.

2. Then the heavens were (being) opened before Jesus.

3. Rightly all creation will have praised (will praise) the innocence of the Lamb.

4. The hall had resounded with the joy of the people.

5. Now Jesus had told the people to enter into the temple.

6. All the apostles had gathered in the upper room, and there they were glorifying God continuously.

7. In the beginning was the Word, and the Word was with God, and God was the Word. [Jn. i, 1]

8. Because of the first fault of Adam we have Christ the Lord.

9. For Christ will have separated the dead from the living.

10. Because of Easter the sorrowful are made joyful.

11. In Judea the apostle had prepared the way of the Lord.

12. They who will always and diligently have worked for the Lord will have an eternal reward in the kingdom of heaven.

13. The little ones, who had come to Jesus in the house of Peter, were being blessed.

14. But a year before, Paul had seen Peter in Galilee.

15. The little servant, who had prepared the meal, knew all who were being called.

16. Paul, a famous teacher in Judea, had known the Scriptures well.

17. The people, who will have gathered in the hall, will rejoice in the victory of Christ.

18. The disciples gathered in the upper room, and Peter said, "Today is a great feast of the Lord."

19. But Paul said to the people, "I am unworthy to be even a slave of our Lord Jesus Christ."

20. For the minister and servants will have bowed [inclined themselves] and will have prayed to God the Lord of creation.

21. What prophet had warned the people in the sacred writings?

22. From here the minister consecrated (will consecrate) the host.

23. The deacon had said, "Paul, whose power was of God, had not been one of the first apostles."

24. According to the Scriptures, blessed will be they forever, who will have observed the commandments of the Lord.

25. The host will be sanctified and will be made a meal of eternal life, because to our minister God has given the power.

26. But it was the third hour. [Mk. xv, 25]

27. Jesus says/said to her: "Well have you said: 'I do not have a husband'; for you have had five husbands, and now, the one whom you have, he is not your husband. This truly you have said." [Jn. iv, 17–18] [Note: In this sentence, as often happens in Scripture, **dicit** is a historical present, ordinarily translated as a simple past. See ahead in Collins, p. 318, section 175.]

II.   1. Scīverāsne innocentiam Agnī?

2. Ad victōriam Filiī multitūdō angelōrum in caelīs exsultāverit.

3. Tertius minister Paulō dīxit, Quoniam audīvimus quia es ēlēctus Deī.

4. Jam Paulus, vir contrītus et dolōrōsus, potentiam Dominī vīderit.

5. In caelō servī Verbī erunt laetī, quod glōriam Dominī scīverint.

Unit 12

Drillə

I. a. vidēre potest: "he/she/it is able to see / can see"
        vidēre possunt: "they are able to see / can see"

    b. audīre poterāmus: "we were able to hear / could hear"
        audīre poteram: "I was able to hear / could hear"

    c. scīre poterunt: "they will be able to know"
        scīre poterit: "he/she/it will be able to know"

    d. parāre potuērunt: "they have been able to provide"
        parāre potuit: "he/she/it has been able to provide"

    e. fīnīre possumus: "we are able to finish / can finish"
        fīnīre possum: "I am able to finish / can finish"

    f. reclīnāre potuerant: "they had been able to lean back"
        reclīnāre potuerat: "he/she/it had been able to lean back"

II. tollō, tollere, sustulī, sublātus

sublātus (-a, -um) sum	sublātī (-ae, -a) sumus
sublātus (-a, -um) es	sublātī (-ae, -a) estis
sublātus (-a, -um) est	sublātī (-ae, -a) sunt

fīniō, fīnīre, fīnīvī (fīniī), fīnītus

fīnītus (-a, -um) sum	fīnītī (-ae, -a) sumus
fīnītus (-a, -um) es	fīnītī (-ae, -a) estis
fīnītus (-a, -um) est	fīnītī (-ae, -a) sunt

aperiō, aperīre, aperuī, apertus

apertus (-a, -um) sum	apertī (-ae, -a) sumus
apertus (-a, -um) es	apertī (-ae, -a) estis
apertus (-a, -um) est	apertī (-ae, -a) sunt

videō, vidēre, vīdī, vīsus

vīsus (-a, -um) sum	vīsī (-ae, -a) sumus
vīsus (-a, -um) es	vīsī (-ae, -a) estis
vīsus (-a, -um) est	vīsī (-ae, -a) sunt

ērigō, ērigere, ērēxī, ērēctus

ērēctus (-a, -um) sum	ērēctī (-ae, -a) sumus
ērēctus (-a, -um) es	ērēctī (-ae, -a) estis
ērēctus (-a, -um) est	ērēctī (-ae, -a) sunt

sānō, sānāre, sānāvī, sānātus

sānātus (-a, -um) sum	sānātī (-ae, -a) sumus
sānātus (-a, -um) es	sānātī (-ae, -a) estis
sānātus (-a, -um) est	sānātī (-ae, -a) sunt

III.   a. mittere debēmus: "we ought to send"

b. esse dēsiit: "he/she/it (has) ceased to be"

c. laudāre potuerat: "he/she/it had been able to praise"

d. miscēre valēbās: "you (sg.) were able to mix"

e. intrāre valēbunt: "they will be able to enter"

f. crēdere vidēminī: "you (pl.) seem to believe"

g. regere potuistis: "you (pl.) have been able to rule"

h. invocāre dēbēbās: "you (sg.) ought to have invoked" [Note that English idiom achieves the past tense of *ought* by using the perfect form of the infinitive complement.]

i. audīre dēsinam: "I will cease to hear"

j. cantāre puerō permittēbat: "he/she/it was permitting the boy to sing"

k. gregāre populō permittit: "he/she/it permits the people to gather"

l. scīre vidēbantur: "they seemed to know"

Exercises

I.   1. Through the power of Jesus Peter was able to forgive the people's debts.

2. Now you send away your servant. [Lk. ii, 29]

3. Certainly we will not cease to praise God. For he is the Lord forever. Amen.

4. After Paul (had) left the hall, he came under the roof of the disciple.

5. Eve was given to Adam by God.

6. After Christ Jesus rose up from the dead, he was seen alive in Galilee by certain disciples.

7. Peter allowed the boy to send food and wine to the family.

8. Before the minister prayed the collect, he bowed in silence.

9. Although sent away by Peter, the man nevertheless kept crying out to Jesus.

10. Before the apostles were left by Jesus, they received power over sin.

11. Because Jesus gave salutary words to the disciples, we ought to pray to God with joy.

12. They will be able to know about the life of the people, but you (pl.) will know about the glory of God.

13. Certain disciples, (who were) not too welcomed, left Galilee.

14. The contrite people, well advised by Paul, began to live according to the precepts of Jesus.

15. In the liturgy the mercy of the Lord was often praised by the people.

16. The beloved apostle knew (how) to write wonderful things about the life of Jesus.

17. Now Eve had conceived her first son.

18. Today we Christians have come together before the table of the Lord.

19. The master saved the best wine till now.

20. The universe has always been governed by the salutary power of God.

21. The disciples therefore seemed certain to take a reward.

22. The wicked servant, warned by the good (one), ceased to curse his master too much.

23. At that time was the best and greatest man governing Judea?

24. The boy suddenly took back the gold, which he had given to Peter, and gave (it) to his family.

25. In Jesus the words of the ancient prophets have been fulfilled.

26. Blessed are those who are able to help the little ones gathered before the house.

27. And the chains of all have been broken. [Acts xvi, 26]

28. To him glory and power forever and ever. Amen. [Rev. i, 6]

29. Amen, amen I say to you: The hour is coming, and it is now. [Jn. v, 25]

30. To you has been given the mystery of the kingdom of God. [Mk. iv, 11]

31. Behold, I see the heavens opened. [Acts vii, 56]

II.   1. Poteritne audīre et agere verba Jēsū?

2. Servus ad ecclēsiam Deī ā Paulō missus est.

3. Hodiē discipulī laetī laudāre maximam potentiam vīvī Deī nōn dēsinent.

4. Servus parvulus scīre parāre Paulō optimam cēnam nōn vidētur.

5. Secundum Scrīptūrās Deus ūnigenitō filiō dēlēre culpam Adae permīsit.

Unit 13

Drills

I. a. cantātus erit: "he/it [e.g., masc. *psalmus*] will have been sung"
      cantātī erunt: "they will have been sung"

   b. data erant: "they had been given"
      datum erat: "it had been given"

   c. laudātī fuerint: "they will have been praised"
      laudātus fuerit: "he/it will have been praised"

   d. sacrāta erat: "she had been made holy"
      sacrātae erant: "they had been made holy"

   e. eritis vocātae: "you (pl. fem.) will have been called"
      eris vocāta: "you (sg. fem.) will have been called"

   f. ductī erāmus: "we had been led"
      ductus eram: "I had been led"

   g. sānāta eris: "you (sg. fem.) will have been healed"
      sānātae eritis: "you (pl. fem.) will have been healed"

   h. corrēctī fuerāmus: "we had been corrected"
      corrēctus fueram: "I had been corrected"

   i. erit fōrmātum: "it will have been trained"
      erunt fōrmāta: "they will have been trained"

   j. satiātae erunt: "they will have been nourished"
      satiāta erit: "she will have been nourished"

45

      k. vīsus eram: "I had been seen / had seemed"
          vīsī erāmus: "we had been seen / had seemed"

      l. missus erō: "I will have been sent"
          missī erimus: "we will have been sent"

II.   a. he had been abandoned: relictus erat

      b. we will have been sent: missī (-ae) erimus

      c. they had been opened: apertī (-ae, -a) erant

      d. you (sg.) will have been seen: vīsus (-a) eris

      e. I had been separated: separātus (-a) eram

      f. I will have been helped: adjūtus (-a) ero

      g. you (pl.) had been guided: fōrmātī (-ae) erātis

      h. they will have been known: scītī (-ae, -a) erunt

      i. she had been strengthened: firmāta erat

      j. he will have been healed: sānātus erit

III.   a. stēllā vīsā: "with the star having been seen"

      b. missō puerō: "with the boy having been sent"

      c. mēnsā praeparātā: "with the table having been prepared"

      d. librīs captīs: "with the books having been taken"

      e. relictā domō: "with the house having been abandoned"

      f. pāpā laudātō: "with the pope having been praised"

      g. populō congregātō: "with the people having been gathered"

      h. solūtīs dēbitīs: "with the debts having been paid back"

      i. laetīs satiātīs: "with the joyful (ones) having been nourished"

      j. īnfirmīs autem sānātīs: "but with the sick having been healed"

Exercises

[Note: Sentences 1, 8, 12, 14, and 25 below contain ablative absolutes. These constructions, extremely flexible in meaning, require a larger context for interpretation. In the first sentence, for example, the ablative absolute could mean "when the hymn was said" or "since the hymn was said" or "although the hymn was said" or even "if the hymn was said." In other words, the circumstance identified by the ablative absolute could be temporal, causal, concessive, or conditional. The whole sentence would need a context for you to decide which sense is the most likely. Following Collins's advice (p. 104), this key uses the formulaic translation indicated in Drill III above, but whenever you see an ablative absolute in an isolated sentence, you may find it fruitful to run through the four principal possibilities of translation.]

I.
1. With the hymn having been said, the apostles left the house.

2. Before the boy was sent to supper, he worked first with all the servants in the field of the Lord.

3. At that time the Galileans were often despised by the Romans, because they did not worship the gods of the Romans.

4. When the words of Jesus will have been heard / are heard, what man will not believe? [Note: For the alternative, idiomatic English translation of conditional future perfects, see ahead in Collins, p. 175.]

5. While he worked, he was praying. [See vocabulary note on **dum** in Collins, p. 107]

6. If my commands will have been observed / are observed by the people, they will have eternal life.

7. Peter will tell the wonders of the Lord to the people, until Paul will have arrived / arrives.

8. With the star having been seen in the sky, the men came from the fields and worshipped the child Jesus.

9. As Jesus looked around, the men were sad and said not one word. For they knew that Jesus had said the truth.

10. When my eyes will have seen / see the Lord, I will be able to finish my life.

11. When the angel of the Lord will have been seen / is seen, the trumpet of victory will be heard over all the earth.

12. Even in the desert of Judea the Baptist knew Jesus. For with Jesus having first been spotted, he said: "Behold the lamb of God."

13. Although he is little, the boy stays at home.

14. With the Baptist having been betrayed, Jesus came into Galilee, where he began to preach the gospel to the people.

15. Mary bore a first child, and he was called Jesus.

16. The holy man took the boy by the right (hand) and led him into the house.

17. When the Jews looked at the finger of God in the heavens, joyful they praised (his) power and mercy.

18. In the beginning God created the world and bestowed the gift of life.

19. Was our nature transformed, when the Son was made incarnate?

20. The child had been held in the arms of Mary.

21. After the wicked man hid the gold, he stood in silence at the right (hand) of Peter.

22. The man, who lost (his) life, had been praised by the Jews.

23. The Romans who had been standing around were threatening the boy.

24. Unless my words will have been accomplished / are accomplished, you will not be blessed.

25. With Christians having been found everywhere, Paul, well satisfied, remained in the house of Peter with joy.

26. By/through my fault, by/through my fault, by/through my greatest fault.

27. And the book of the prophet was handed over to Jesus.

28. He is not here, but he has arisen. [Lk. xxiv, 6]

II. 1. Cēnā praeparātā / Postquam cēna praeparāta erat, Petrus novō discipulō astāre ad dexteram Paulī permīsit.

2. Populus, quī salūtiferīs Christī praeceptīs monitus erat, poterat orāre Deum, quī ūniversum rēgnat.

3. Cum Paulus ad domum advēnerit, ā Petrō Galilaeō vidēbitur.

4. Postquam apostolus puerum secundum sānāvit, servus laudāre misericordiam Deī nōn dēsiit.

Unit 14

Drills

I. a. hominī: dative singular ("for/to a/the human being")
        hominibus: dative plural ("for/to [the] human beings")

    b. patre: ablative singular ("from/with/in/by a/the father")
        patribus: ablative plural ("from/with/in/by [the] fathers")

    c. redēmptōrum: genitive plural ("of [the] redeemers")
        redēmptōris: genitive singular ("of a/the redeemer")

    d. regis: genitive singular ("of a/the king")
        regum: genitive plural ("of [the] kings)

    e. sacerdōtibus: dative plural ("for/to [the] priests")
        sacerdōtī: dative singular ("for/to a/the priest")

        sacerdōtibus: ablative plural ("from/with/in/by [the] priests")
        sacerdōte: ablative singular ("from/with/in/by a/the priest")

    f. dēprecātiōnēs: nominative plural ("[the] supplications")
        dēprecātiō: nominative singular ("a/the supplication")

        dēprecātiōnēs: accusative plural ("[the] supplications")
        dēprecātiōnem: accusative singular ("a/the supplication")

    g. mātrem: accusative singular ("a/the mother")
        mātrēs: accusative plural ("[the] mothers")

h. ōrātiōne: ablative singular ("from/with/in/by a/the prayer")
   ōrātiōnibus: ablative plural ("from/with/in/by [the] prayers")

i. pācem: accusative singular ("a/the peace")
   pācēs: accusative plural ("[the] peaces")

j. virginibus: dative plural ("for/to [the] virgins")
   virginī: dative singular ("for/to a/the virgin")

   virginibus: ablative plural ("from/with/in/by [the] virgins)
   virgine: ablative singular ("from/with/in/by a/the virgin")

k. voluntātum: genitive plural ("of [the] wills")
   voluntātis: genitive singular ("of a/the will")

l. patris: genitive singular ("of a/the father")
   patrum: genitive plural ("of [the] fathers")

m. rēx: nominative singular ("a/the king")
   rēgēs: nominative plural ("[the] kings")

n. ōrātiō: nominative singular ("a/the prayer")
   ōrātiōnēs: nominative plural ("[the] prayers")

o. sacerdōtī: dative singular ("for/to a/the priest")
   sacerdōtibus: dative plural ("for/to [the] priests")

II. a. baptisma: nominative or accusative singular ("a/the baptism")
        baptismata: nominative or accusative plural ("[the] baptisms")

     b. corpora: nominative or accusative plural ("[the] bodies")
        corpus: nominative or accusative singular ("a/the body")

     c. generibus: dative plural ("for/to [the] nations")
        generī: dative singular ("for/to a/the nation")

        generibus: ablative plural ("from/with/in/by [the] nations")
        genere: ablative singular ("from/with/in/by a/the nation")

     d. lūminis: genitive singular ("of a/the light")
        lūminum: genitive plural ("of [the] lights")

     e. mūnera: nominative or accusative plural ("[the] gifts")
        mūnus: nominative or accusative singular ("a/the gift")

f. nōmine: ablative singular ("from/with/in/by a/the name")
    nōminibus: ablative plural ("from/with/in/by [the] names")

g. genera: nominative or accusative plural ("[the] nations")
    genus: nominative or accusative singular ("a/the nation")

h. lūminī: dative singular ("for/to a/the light")
    lūminibus: dative plural ("for/to [the] lights")

i. baptismatum: genitive plural ("of [the] baptisms")
    baptismatis: genitive singular ("of a/the baptism")

j. mūneribus: dative plural ("for/to [the] gifts")
    mūnerī: dative singular ("for/to a/the gift")

    mūneribus: ablative plural ("from/with/in/by [the] gifts")
    mūnere: ablative singular ("from/with/in/by a/the gift")

Exercises

I. 1. Although the chief priest heard the words of Jesus, he nevertheless adhered to the old ways, and he did not believe.

2. In the temple Jesus read a prayer from the book of the prophet.

3. Therefore the apostles gathered food and gave (it) to the people.

4. With the book having been written, the apostle again came to the land where he had been chosen by Jesus many years before.

5. You know that John was called the beloved disciple.

6. If our prayer will have been accepted by the Father, we will be happy.

7. The sorrowful mother received the body of Jesus in (her) arms; afterwards the body was hidden in the ground.

8. Saint Peter, a man of peace and good will, was selected chief of all the apostles.

9. Our sins have been washed away by the Redeemer, Jesus Christ.

10. The new disciple, although he was not one of the apostles, wrote the gospel for all human beings.

11. The disciple's Gospel of Jesus Christ was always read through all lands. For he described the life of Jesus in the book.

12. At that time the family of Jesus came to Bethlehem and was enrolled.

13. After John was betrayed, Jesus began (his) ministry.

14. Because of the king, a man of wicked spirit, the family left the land of (their) fathers.

15. After our priest read the prayer, we added: "Amen."

16. Mary, both virgin and mother, (is) praised by all human beings.

17. The holy family lived in the land of Egypt for many years, while the wicked king ruled in Galilee.

18. With the name of Jesus having been spoken by the priest, the people bowed.

19. Where there is light, there is life.

20. God from God, light from light, true God from true God . . .

21. And so we have called upon the Father and we have given great thanks to the Son.

22. The Jews were freed from (their) sins by the baptism of John.

23. By the First Testament of God the Jewish nation was made a light for all the world.

24. The Hebrews were guided by the Lord on a dry path through the water.

25. Gold and swords, gifts of the people, had already been given to the king.

26. After Paul wrote to the Romans, the disciple was able to prepare a meal for Paul.

27. This is Jesus, King of the Jews. [Mt. xxvii, 37]

28. And behold, the heavens were opened to Jesus. [Mt. iii, 16]

II.   1. Sacerdōs noster, vir pācis, rēgēs Chrīstiānōs et prīncipēs orāvit.

2. Secundum Jōannem, Jēsūs est rēx glōriae et redēmptor hominum.

3. Jōannēs astitit cum Rōmānī corpus Jēsū mātrī Marīae dedērunt.

4. Sī nōmen Patris invocāmus, dēprecātiōnem nostram semper accipit.

5. Quamquam puer, fīlius rēgis, ā sacerdōte fōrmābātur, nōn tamen nimis inhaesit mandātīs Deī.

Unit 15

Drills

I. a. ambōnis: genitive singular ("of a/the lectern")
       ambōnum: genitive plural ("of [the] lecterns")

    b. pānis: nominative singular ("a/the bread")
       pānēs: nominative plural ("[the] breads")

       pānis: genitive singular ("of a/the bread")
       pānium: genitive plural ("of [the] breads")

    c. postium: genitive plural ("of [the] doorposts")
       postis: genitive singular ("of a/the doorpost")

    d. sanguine: ablative singular ("from/with/in/by a/the blood")
       sanguinibus: ablative plural ("from/with/in/by [the] bloods")

    e. fīnēs: nominative plural ("[the] ends")
       fīnis: nominative singular ("a/the end")

       fīnēs: accusative plural ("[the] ends")
       fīnem: accusative singular ("a/the end")

    f. mentium: genitive plural ("of [the] minds")
       mentis: genitive singular ("of a/the mind")

    g. lēctiōnī: dative singular ("for/to a/the reading")
       lēctiōnibus: dative plural ("for/to [the] readings")

    h. cordis: genitive singular ("of a/the heart")
       cordium: genitive plural ("of [the] hearts")

i. maria: nominative or accusative plural ("[the] seas")
    mare: nominative or accusative singular ("a/the sea")

j. marī: dative singular ("for/to a/the sea")
    maribus: dative plural ("for/to [the] seas")

    marī: ablative singular ("from/with/in/by a/the sea")
    maribus: ablative plural ("from/with/in/by [the] seas")

k. salūtibus: dative plural ("for/to [the] safeties")
    salūtī: dative singular ("for/to a/the safety")

    salūtibus: ablative plural ("from/with/in/by [the] safeties")
    salūte: ablative singular ("from/with/in/by a/the safety)

l. inīquitās: nominative singular ("a/the wickedness")
    inīquitātēs: nominative plural ("[the] wickednesses")

m. cruōrem: accusative singular ("a/the blood")
    cruōrēs: accusative plural ("[the] bloods")

n. mortēs: nominative plural ("[the] deaths")
    mōrs: nominative singular ("a/the death")

    mortēs: accusative plural ("[the] deaths")
    mortem: accusative singular ("a/the death")

o. cālīgō: nominative singular ("a/the mist")
    cālīginēs: nominative plural ("[the] mists")

II. a. They are making the man (their) prince.

     b. We are calling Jesus (our) king.

     c. We consider Peter good.

     d. God created the world good.

     e. They (have) elected John (as) pope.

     f. John Paul was elected pope.

Exercises

I.   1. Many of the men healed by Jesus did not give thanks to God.

2. John prepared the way of the Lord; many of the Jews, contrite of heart, received baptism of water from John; Jesus also came to John for baptism; according to John we ought to call Jesus the Lamb of God.

3. At the end of the age the trumpet of justice will have sounded.

4. At first the reader will read the first reading at the lectern; from there the cantor will sing a song.

5. The blood of the lamb on the doorposts made the ancient He brews safe.

6. At Easter we are joyful, because through the resurrection of the Redeemer we have been made partakers of a new life.

7. The Hebrews, whose hearts were fit for the ministry of the Lord, were led through the Red Sea.

8. The gloom of wickedness is put to flight; the light of Christ is seen by all human beings. Alleluia.

9. Beyond all persons we praise Mary, Star of the Sea, because she is the Mother of God.

10. Unless you will have eaten /eat my body and will have drunk / drink my blood, you will not enter into the kingdom of heaven.

    [Note: See ahead to Collins, p. 175, for the normal, idiomatic translation of conditional future perfects.]

11. With the blood of the lamb having been seen on the doorposts of the Hebrews, the angel of God did not enter into the houses (lit.: under the roofs). [Note: Review ablative absolute in Collins, p. 104; see also #28 and #29 below.]

12. Because of Christ's victory over death the hall resounded with joyful hymns.

13. Did the crowd have enough bread? Unless they will have eaten / eat enough, some of the people will fail on the road.

14. Did Peter first call Jesus the Christ? Although Peter did not know much, he saw that Jesus was the Lord.

15. Are the men, trained by the deacon, now suitable for baptism?

16. John, nearest to the heart of Jesus, stood by at the right (hand) of Mary.

17. At the death of Jesus the apostles, because they were human, were made sad; but at the resurrection, (they were made) happy.

18. Jesus, redeemer of the human race, is praised before all every where.

19. Even if we are not always able to know the mind of God, the good trust in the Lord.

20. Through the generosity of the good Lord, our table is full of food.

21. Even some of the best human beings have been deceived by evil.

22. Have you heard that all creatures first came from the sea?

23. After a reading of the Gospel the people cried out a response.

24. We humans, who live in the world, praise the Father, who founded the world.

25. The Roman bishop, even though a good and just person, did not live a sufficiently blessed life.

26. We call Mary the Queen of Heaven, because she is the Mother of God.

27. We will always and everywhere hold in mind the mercy of the Lord.

28. With the eternal food having been eaten, we add a prayer before the end of Mass.

29. With Galilee having been left behind, Jesus again came to the district of Judea with (his) apostles.

30. The Lord raises our minds to heavenly desires.

31. Blessed (are those) with pure heart, because they will see God. [Mt. v, 8]

32. We worship what we know, because salvation is from the Jews. [Jn. iv, 22]

II. 1. Laetī sumus quoniam Jēsūs, Fīlius ūnigenitus Patris, est particeps nostrae nātūrae hūmānae.

2. Multī Galilaeōrum nōn scīverant quia Deus Marīam mātrem Jēsū ēlēgit.

3. Cantor canticum satis grātum populō cantāvit.

4. Vocāvēruntne multī Jūdaeōrum Deum Rēgem Rēgum?

Unit 16

Drills

I. A. omnis, omne "every, all"

1. omnis homō: nominative singular ("every person")
    omnēs hominēs: nominative plural ("all [the] persons")

2. nōminis omnis: genitive singular ("of every name")
    nōminum omnium: genitive plural ("of all [the] names")

3. omnem lēctiōnem: accusative singular ("every reading")
    omnēs lēctiōnēs: accusative plural ("all [the] readings")

4. omnibus baptismatibus: dative plural ("for/to all [the] baptisms")
    omnī baptismatī: dative singular ("for/to every baptism")

    omnibus baptismatibus: ablative plural ("from/with/in/by all [the] baptisms)
    omnī baptismate: ablative singular ("from/with/in/by every baptism")

5. omnī ecclēsiae: dative singular ("for/to every church")
    omnibus ecclēsiīs: dative plural ("for/to all [the] churches")

6. omnēs pāpae: nominative plural ("all [the] popes")
    omnis pāpa: nominative singular ("every pope")

7. angelō omnī: dative singular ("for/to every angel")
    angelīs omnibus: dative plural ("for/to all [the] angels")

angelō omnī: ablative singular ("from/with/in/by every
  angel")
angelīs omnibus: ablative plural ("from/with/in/by all [the]
  angels")

8. omnium apostolōrum: genitive plural ("of all [the] apostles")
    omnis apostolī: genitive singular ("of every apostle")

9. omnī Missā: ablative singular ("from/with/in/by every
    Mass")
    omnibus Missīs: ablative plural ("from/with/in/by all [the]
    Masses")

10. omnia mandāta: nominative/accusative plural ("all [the]
    commandments")
    omne mandātum: nominative/accusative singular
    ("every commandment")

B. ācer, ācris, ācre "bitter"

1. servus ācer: nominative singular ("a/the bitter servant")
    servī ācrēs: nominative plural ("[the] bitter servants")

2. rēgīna ācris: nominative singular ("a/the bitter queen")
    rēgīnae ācrēs: nominative plural ("[the] bitter queens")

3. ācris rēgīnae: genitive singular ("of a/the bitter queen")
    ācrium rēgīnārum: genitive plural ("of [the] bitter queens")

4. ācrī diācōnō: dative singular ("for/to a/the bitter deacon")
    ācribus diācōnīs: dative plural ("for/to [the] bitter deacons")

    ācrī diācōnō: ablative singular ("from/with/in/by a/the bitter
    deacon")
    ācribus diācōnīs: ablative plural ("from/with/in/by [the]
    bitter deacons")

5. dōnum ācre: nominative/accusative singular: ("a/the
    bitter gift")
    dōna ācria: nominative/accusative plural ("[the] bitter gifts")

C. fēlīx (*gen.*, fēlīcis) "happy"

1. fēlīcī famīliae: dative singular ("for/to a/the happy family")
   fēlīcibus famīliīs: dative plural ("for/to [the] happy families")

2. famīliae fēlīcis: genitive singular ("of a/the happy family")
   familiārum fēlīcium: genitive plural ("of [the] happy families")

3. fēlīcēs discipulōs: accusative plural ("[the] happy disciples")
   fēlīcem discipulum: accusative singular ("a/the happy disciple")

4. fēlīx rēgnum: nominative/accusative singular ("a/the happy kingdom")
   fēlīcia rēgna: nominative/accusative plural ("[the] happy kingdoms")

5. saecula fēlīcia: nominative/accusative plural ("[the] happy ages")
   saeculum fēlīx: nominative/accusative singular ("a/the happy age")

II. 1. Paulus vīdit Petrum *ambulantem* in viā.
     Paul saw Peter *walking* on the road.

   2. *Vidēns* Jēsūm, vir clāmāvit.
      Seeing Jesus, the man cried out.

   3. Beātī quī, *audientēs,* verbum Dominī faciunt.
      Blessed (are those) who, *hearing,* do the word of the Lord.

   4. Servus cēnam parābat Paulō *venientī* in domum.
      The servant was preparing a meal for Paul (as he was) *coming* into the house.

   5. Ōrāmus prō in Dominō *vīventibus.*
      We pray for (those who are) *living* in the Lord.

   6. Paulus vocāvit ūnum hominum ex ecclēsiā *venientium.*
      Paul called one of the people (who were) *coming* out of the church.

Exercises

I.   1. In the name of the Father and of the Son and of the Holy Spirit.
          Amen.

      2. And my blood is the true drink. [Jn. vi, 55]

      3. The apostles gave the wonderful bread(s) to the people reclined
          on the ground.

      4. Your body is a temple of the Holy Spirit, who is in you, whom
          you have from God, and you are not your own. [I Cor. vi, 19]

      5. Then Jesus and the apostles were within the house, eating the
          Paschal supper. But one had already betrayed the Lord.

      6. The little maidservant, approaching Jesus, said with innocence:
          "I know that you are able to heal (those) being sick / those who
          are sick. Will you not heal my mother?" And Jesus entered the
          house and healed the mother of the maidservant.

      7. a. But while Jesus walked to the sea, he saw Peter. [Review
              Collins, p. 107.]

          b. But while Jesus was walking to the sea, he saw Peter.

          c. But Jesus, (while) walking to the sea, saw Peter teaching the
              happy people.

      8. And all the people saw him walking and praising God.
          [Acts iii, 9]

      9. But the disciples collected the bread broken in pieces / the
          fragments of bread (which had been) left behind by the people.

     10. Glory (be) to the Father and to the Son and to the Holy Spirit.

     11. He took the bread and giving thanks broke (it) and said: *"This is
          my body."* [I Cor. xi, 23–24]

     12. *"This cup is the new covenant in my blood."* [I Cor. xi, 25]

     13. For Christ Jesus poured out (his) blood for the life of the world.

     14. But we have not received the spirit of the world, but the Spirit,
          which is from God. [I Cor. ii, 12]

15. Kneeling in prayer, we will always praise the Lord, who made the world saved / saved the world by (his) passion and death on the cross and resurrection.

16. But with the wine (having been) poured into the cup, Jesus blessed (it) and gave (it) to (his) apostles, saying: "This is my blood. If you drink (it), you will live forever." [Review Collins, p. 104, on the ablative absolute. Notice too, once again, that the future perfect in a conditional clause is best translated as a simple present in English, thus also indicating a time frame antecedent to the future tense in the concluding clause.]

17. Who will separate us from the love of Christ? [Rom. viii, 35]

18. But Jesus, mindful of (his) omnipotent Father, went up into the temple and looked at the faces of (those who were) praying. And within the temple he found many, both happy and ardent.

19. Mindful of the Paschal rite, we see the sweetness and the mercy and the love of God the Father.

20. And Peter found Jesus on the mountaintop praying for all human beings.

21. The Son of man came eating and drinking. [Mt. xi, 19]

22. But the souls of the just are in the hand of God. [Wisdom iii, 1]

23. Wherefore happy we have heard the saving precept of the Lord, and we love all, both (those who are) similar to us and (those who are) dissimilar.

24. Jesus, reclined in the upper room, was breaking bread with the apostles.

25. Through all the ages of ages / Forever and ever.

II.   1. Quamquam omnēs mandūcāverant, nōn tamen erant fēlīcēs.

2. Cum ad Patrem ascenderit, Jēsūs virōs nōn audientēs verba Patris cōnfundētur. [Review the vocabulary note on **cōnfundō** in Collins, p. 131.]

3. Cruce et resurrēctiōne Jēsūs mundum salvum fēcit.

4. Capiēns manū virum īnfirmum, Petrus in domum indūxit, ubi virō pōtum vīnī dēdit.

5. Memorēs culpārum nostrārum, laudāmus misericordiam Dominī vīvī.

Unit 17

Drills

I. 1. I wish to do the Pasch with my disciples.

2. Do you (sg.) wish to do the Pasch?

3. Paul wishes to come to the house of Peter.

4. We want bread, not wine.

5. Do you (pl.) wish to hear the reading?

6. The apostles wish to leave Paul behind.

7. The deacon wanted to see the bishop.

8. Will the deacon want to see the bishop?

9. The people wanted the priest to fulfill the rite.

10. Why did you (sg.) want to come to the sea?

II. 1. I go / am going to my Father.

2. Are you (sg.) going away from / leaving the temple?

3. Peter goes / is going in to the apostles.

4. We go / are going out of the house.

5. Were you (pl.) going into Galilee?

6. The men are going out from the church.

7. They will go to Jerusalem.

8. Are you Christians going to Rome?

9. They went into the hall.

10. I wish to go home.

Exercises

I.   1. After the crowds ate enough, the apostles went and collected all the bread(s) left behind.

   2. For he who will have wished / wishes to save his own life, he will lose it; but he who will have lost / loses his own life on account of me and the gospel, he will save it. [Mk. viii, 35]

   3. It is truly worthy and just to proclaim the invisible God the Father almighty and his only begotten Son, our Lord Jesus Christ.

   4. a. Jesus went into the world for the remission of our sins, and was crucified for all.

      b. Jesus, who went into the world for the remission of our sins, was crucified for all human beings.

      c. Jesus the Savior, going into the world for the remission of sins, did the will of (his) merciful Father.

   5. O the love of charity! For our Father sent his only begotten Son.

   6. I believe in one God, the Father almighty, maker of heaven and of earth, of all (things) visible and invisible.

   7. As suppliants, therefore, we wish to make an acceptable sacrifice to the Lord of goodness.

   8. The angel of the Lord announced to Mary: "You will be the Mother of God."

9. But with Paul willing / Though Paul wanted to go in among the people, the disciples did not allow (him to do so). [Acts xix, 30. Review the ablative absolute in Collins, p. 104.]

10. The books of the Old Testament and of the New, many in number, are advantageous to all (those) believing in God.

11. Jesus was walking around Galilee, and he was teaching the people. Afterwards he went back to Jerusalem, where he spoke to the apostles about death and resurrection.

12. But Judas too, who was betraying him, knew the place. [Jn. xviii, 2]

13. It is written in the book of the Old Testament first that God sent out (his) spirit and brought Adam to life.

14. The deacon, pouring out prayers for the people, diligently accomplished (his) praise of the candle.

15. Paul, declaring the glorious coming of the Son, was confusing the Jews who were present in the temple.

16. Saint Peter, servant and apostle of Jesus Christ, first held the episcopal power in Rome.

17. I therefore want the men to pray in every place. [I Tim. ii, 8]

18. Our bread, fruit of the earth, blessed by the priest, will be the bread of eternal life for all.

19. With God willing, all nature will be purified (will have been purified).

20. Because of the happy fault of Adam, Jesus came into the world and reconciled to the Father all the sons of Adam.

21. The apostles, sent off by Jesus, were able to cure the sick and to forgive sins.

22. But Peter and John were going up into the temple at the hour of prayer, the ninth (hour). [Acts iii, 1]

II. 1. Postquam Petrus ā Rōmā abīvit, vēnit in Hierosolymam, quoniam vidēre Paulum dē cibō mundō et immundō voluit.

2. Paulus vult ad templum īre et nūntiāre Dominum Jēsūm, quia est Fīlius Deī.

3. Athēnīs nōn admissum est / fuit Paulum inīre ad populum.

4. Paulus, quamquam prīncipem sacerdōtum in Jerūsalem cōnfundēbat, tamen voluit abīre et nūntiāre populō Rōmae adventum Salvātōris.

Unit 18

Drills

I.   1. dō, dare, dedī, datus
   datūrus, -a, -um: "about to give"
   dandus, -a, -um: "having to be given"

     2. dēleō, dēlēre, dēlēvī, dēlētus
   dēlētūrus, -a, -um: "about to destroy"
   dēlendus, -a, -um: "having to be destroyed"

     3. agō, agere, ēgī, āctus
   āctūrus, -a, -um: "about to do"
   agendus, -a, -um: "having to be done"

     4. suscipiō, suscipere, suscēpi, susceptus
   susceptūrus, -a, -um: "about to take up"
   suscipiendus, -a, -um: "having to be taken up"

     5. fīniō, fīnīre, fīnīvī (fīniī), fīnītus
   fīnītūrus, -a, -um: "about to end"
   fīniendus, -a, um: "having to be ended"

     6. extollō, extollere, extulī, —
   [no perfect passive base available to form future active participle]
   extollendus, -a, -um: "having to be lifted up"

II. 1. Christ is about to come with glory.

2. Mary was about to pray.

3. The deacon had been about to read the first reading.

4. The first reading will have to be read by the deacon.

5. The wine must be mixed by the servant.

6. The bread(s) had to be gathered up by the apostles.

Exercises

I. 1. Whoever does the law according to the will of the Father is going to arrive at eternal glory in the kingdom of heaven.

2. With the rite (having been) begun, the devout gather around the Lord's festive altar, made by the art of humanity. [Review the ablative absolute in Collins, p. 104.]

3. I have not come to break up (abolish) the Law or the Prophets; I have not come to abolish (them), but to fulfill (them). [Mt. v, 17]

4. The kind Father always gives daily bread to humanity.

5. After the ascension of Jesus, the apostles stood by in Galilee, looking into the heavens.

6. With the first reading having been read, the beginning of the Gospel according to Luke had to be read by the deacon. With the reading finished, the people cried out.

7. But the man, looking intently at Jesus, cried aloud: "You can save me. Will you therefore grant your mercy to an unworthy person?"

8. The wisdom and mercy of God must be praised by all Christians always and everywhere.

9. Even though walking in the darkness, we nevertheless have Christ, the unfailing light. And he always shows the way to (his) people. [Review the connective relative in Collins, p. 84.]

10. The Lord Jesus would often explain to the apostles that his death was going to be enough for the salvation of the world.

11. When Jesus descended from the mountain and came upon (them), he immediately began to explain to the apostles (his) death (about) to come / (his) approaching death.

12. But Jesus did not wish to go around in Judea, because the Jews were saying that he had to be killed.

13. When the apostles were shut up in the upper room, Jesus, with the chains of death broken, approached (them) and said: "Behold I am present."

14. And Jesus, baptized, immediately went up from the water. [Mt. iii, 16]

15. With the Mass begun, the priest used to say: I will go to the altar of God.

16. John the Baptist said that he should have been baptized by Jesus.

17. But after I will have arisen again / rise again, I will go before you into Galilee. [Mt. xxvi, 32]

18. Then the priest, with his hands extended, says a prayer.

19. And looking at Jesus walking, he says: "Behold the lamb of God." [Jn. i, 36]

20. We believe in the Holy Spirit, Lord and maker-of-life / the one who makes life, who proceeds from the Father and the Son.

21. The Body of Christ will guard me into eternal life.

22. But I do not find (it possible) to do good completely.

23. From there an angel of the Lord is about to approach shepherds guarding (their) flocks in the fields.

24. For behold, I announce to you great joy, which will be for all people. The Gospel according to Luke ii, 10.

25. I am the Alpha and the Omega, says the Lord God, who is and who was and who is about to come, the Omnipotent. [Rev. i, 8]

26. Blessed (are those) who walk in the law of the Lord.

II.   1. Paulus videndus erit Petrō, quī Rōmam adventūrus est.

2. Grex pāstōrī bonō custōdiendus est.

3. Sacerdōs benīgnus, manibus extēnsīs, prō omnī hūmānitāte ōrātūrus erat.

4. Jēsūs dīxit quia contrītī apostolīs baptizandī erant.

5. Lūcās scīvit quia librum dē Salvātōre scrīptūrus erat.

6. Dēvōtī tenebrās mundī fugātās lūmine indēficientī sapientiae et clēmentiae vidēbunt.

Unit 19

Drills

I.   1. ambulā, fīlī! ("Walk, son!")
ambulāte, fīliī ("Walk, sons!")

2. cantāte, chorī angelōrum! ("Sing, choirs of angels!")
cantā, chore angelōrum! ("Sing, choir of angels!")

3. observāte! ("Watch [pl.]!")
observā! ("Watch [sg.]!")

4. incipite! ("Begin [pl.]!")
incipe! ("Begin [sg.]!")

5. habēminī! ("Be held [pl.]!")
habēre! ("Be held [sg.]!")

6. jungere! ("Be joined [sg.]!")
jungiminī ("Be joined [pl.]!")

7. venī! ("Come [sg.]!")
venīte ("Come [pl.]!")

8. adeste (adestōte), fidēlēs! ("Be present, faithful [ones]!")
ades (adestō), fidēlis! ("Be present, faithful [one]!")

9. dīc! ("Say [sg.]!")
dīcite! ("Say [pl.]!")

fac! ("Do [sg.]!")
facite! ("Do [pl.]!")

10. rege! ("Rule [sg.]!")
    regite! ("Rule [pl.]!")

11. exaudī, Domine! ("Hear favorably, Lord!")
    exaudīte, dominī! ("Hear favorably, masters!")

12. virī, sānāminī! ("Men, be healed!")
    vir, sānāre! ("Man, be healed!")

II.   1. Ego tē videō.
       I see you.

       Nōs vōs vidēmus.
       We see you (pl.).

   2. Tū mē vidēs.
       You see me.

       Vōs nōs vidētis.
       You see us.

   3. Vōs estis memorēs meī?
       Are *you* mindful of me?

       Tū es memor nostrī?
       Are *you* mindful of us?

   4. Nōs ōrāvimus prō vōbis.
       We prayed for you.

       Ego ōrāvī prō tibi.
       I prayed for you.

   5. Tū veniēs mēcum?
       Will *you* come with me?

       Vōs veniētis nōbīscum?
       Will *you* come with us?

   6. Nōs ūnum vestrum ēlēgimus.
       We have chosen one of you.

       Ego ūnum vestrum ēlēgī.
       I have chosen one of you.

7. Vōs mihi librum dedistis?
Have *you* given the book to me?

Tū nōbīs librum dedistī?
Have *you* given the book to us?

8. Laus tibi, Chrīste.
Praise (be) to you, Christ.

9. Propter tuī dīlēctiōnem vēnī ego.
Because of (my) love for you, *I* have come.

Propter vestrī dīlēctiōnem vēnimus nōs.
Because of (our) love for you, *we* have come.

10. Pāx vōbīscum.
Peace (be) with you.

Pāx tēcum.
Peace (be) with you.

Exercises

I.   1. Lamb of God, who take away the sins of the world, grant us peace.

2. Son, your sins are forgiven you. [Mk. ii, 5]

3. Then the beloved apostle told the disciples the things which had occurred in Jerusalem on the second day.

4. But the bread, which *I* will give, is my flesh for the life of the world. [Jn. vi, 51]

5. The Lord (be) with you. And with your spirit.
Upward (be your) hearts. We hold (our hearts) toward the Lord.

6. Caring for us, Jesus was wounded in (his) side and poured out the blood of salvation.

7. Blessed (are) you among women. [Lk. i, 42]

8. And guarding yourselves from these you will do well. [Acts xv, 29. Review the connective relative in Collins, p. 84.]

9. Do you believe in the Son of man? [Jn. ix, 35]

10. Pouring out our prayers, we the faithful desire your salvation for us, O sweet Jesus! Come, Lord Jesus!

11. The just (man) shall live by faith. [Gal. iii, 11]

12. But I wish you to know that Christ is the head of every man, and the man (is) the head of the woman, but God (is) the head of Christ. [I Cor. xi, 3]

13. Leave there your gift before the altar. [Mt. v, 24]

14. But I praise you [, brothers,] because in all respects you are mindful of me. [I Cor. xi, 2]

15. We are nourished daily by your love, O Lord: truly you have taught us your salvation.

16. The woman says to him: "Lord, I see that you are a prophet." [Jn. iv, 19]

17. Give us today our life-sustaining bread. [Mt. vi, 11]

18. I give thanks to my God always for you in the grace of God, which has been given to you in Christ Jesus. [I Cor. i, 4]

19. Lord, teach us to pray, as also John taught his disciples. [Lk. xi, 1]

20. Send her away, because she cries out after us. [Mt. xv, 23]

21. Do you believe that I am able to do this? [Mt. ix, 28]

22. And they chose Stephen, a man full of faith and the Holy Spirit. [Acts vi, 5]

23. The Lord Jesus will do away with (him) by the breath of (his) mouth. [II Thess. ii, 8]

24. If therefore *you* will have worshipped / worship in my presence, all (this) will be yours. [Lk. iv, 7]

25. For my flesh is the true food, and my blood is the true drink. [Jn. vi, 55]

26. But hope which is seen is not hope. [Rom. viii, 24]

27. Jesus said, "Make the people sit down." [Jn. vi, 10]

28. Today this Scripture has been fulfilled in your hearing / ears. [Lk. iv, 21]

29. Having eyes do you not see, and having ears do you not hear? [Mk. viii, 18]

30. Who is my mother and (who are) my brothers? [Mk. iii, 33]

31. Amen I say to you: One of you is about to betray me. [Mt. xxvi, 21]

32. All things have been handed over to me by my Father. [Mt. xi, 27]

33. Jesus therefore said to Peter: "Put (your) sword into (its) scabbard; shall I not drink the cup which the Father has given to me?" [Jn. xviii, 11]

34. Go, the Mass is (over).

35. The Teacher says: " . . . at your house I make the Pasch with my disciples." [Mt. xxvi, 18]

36. Give to us daily our daily bread, and forgive us our sins. [Lk. xi, 3–4]

37. Holy Mary, pray for us.
    Saint Peter, pray for us.
    All you holy Disciples of the Lord, pray for us.
    Christ, hear us.
    Christ, hear us favorably.
    Lord, have mercy.
    Christ, have mercy.
    Lord, have mercy.

II.   1. Domine, docē nōs modōs tuōs.

2. Frātrēs, cadite in genua vestra et adōrāte Dominum.

3. O Domine, donā nōbīs grātiam mortis fēlīcis.

4. Dīlige proximum tuum, mī filī.

5. Cum tē ad templum advēneris, mitte ad mē servum tuum.

6. Mittamne ego digitum meum in latus Dominī?

Unit 20

Drills

I.   1a. admīror, admīrārī, —, admīrātus sum "wonder at"
        admīrāns, admīrantis ("wondering at")
        admīrātus, -a, -um ("having wondered at") [Note the active
            meaning.]
        admīrātūrus, -a, -um ("about to wonder at")
        admīrandus, -a, -um ("having to be wondered at") [Note the
            passive meaning.]

    1b. audeō, audēre, —, ausus sum "dare"
        audēns, audentis ("daring")
        ausus, -a, -um ("having dared") [Note the active meaning.]
        ausūrus, -a, -um ("about to dare")
        audendus, -a, -um ("having to be dared") [Note the passive
            meaning.]

    2a. admīrātur: 3rd sg. present deponent ("he/she/it wonders at")

    2b. admīrābātur: 3rd sg. imperfect deponent ("he/she/it was
        wondering at")

    2c. admīrātus est: 3rd sg. perfect deponent ("he/she/it [has]
        wondered at")

    2d. audet: 3rd sg. present active ("he/she/it dares")

    2e. audēbit: 3rd sg. future active ("he/she/it will dare")

    2f. ausus eram: 1st sg. pluperfect deponent ("I had dared")

II.   a. Laudēmus Dominum.
           Let us praise the Lord.
           Laudāmus Dominum.
           We (are) praise(ing) the Lord.

    b. Līberēmus servōs!
           Let us free the slaves!
           Līberāmus servōs.
           We (are) free(ing) the slaves.

    c. Utinam Deus servet nōs!
           Would that God may keep us!
           Deus servat nōs.
           God keeps / is keeping us.

    d. Tua fidēs firmētur.
           May your faith be strengthened.
           Tua fidēs firmātur.
           Your faith is (being) strengthened.

    e. Vocēmur ad Dominī cēnam!
           May we be called to the supper of the Lord!
           Vocāmur ad Dominī cēnam.
           We are (being) called to the supper of the Lord.

Exercises

I.   1. The Son of man is betrayed into the hands of sinners.
         [Mt. xxvi, 45]

    2. Admonished by salutary commands, we dare to say:

    3. Our Father, you who are in heaven, may your name be sanctified.
         [Mt. vi, 9]

    4. Let us wretched ones beseech the Lord to put our sins to flight!

    5. May the Body and Blood of the Lord Jesus Christ free us from all
       our iniquities.

    6. The crowd wondered at the wonderful works of Jesus.

    7. To the Lord let us give our bread, fruit of the earth and of the
       work of human hands.

8. Peter was amazed that the people trusted not at all in the Lord.

9. May the paternal love always preserve us!

10. Paul, holding in memory the words and works of Jesus, was powerful in preaching the Gospel.

11. It is necessary for the priest to invoke the blessing of the Lord on behalf of the people.

12. The light of the world has arisen and has put to flight the darkness of sinners.

13. The wretched man, pouring out tears, said that his son was dying.

14. He will baptize you in the Holy Spirit and in fire. [Mt. iii, 11]

15. This is the night, which today through all the world returns to grace (those) believing in Christ.

16. …God from God, light from light, true God from true God, begotten, not made, consubstantial with the Father: through whom all things have been made.

17. Therefore I beseech blessed Mary ever Virgin, all the Angels, and the Saints, and you, brothers, to pray for me to the Lord our God.

18. For the Lord Jesus was crucified, suffered and died for the life of the world.

19. O Lord, make me also adhere always to your commandments.

20. There was born to us today a Savior, who is Christ the Lord. [Lk. ii, 11]

21. *I* have baptized you with water; but indeed *he* will baptize you with the Holy Spirit. [Mk. i, 8]

22. Why does your Master eat and drink with sinners?

23. I have sinned betraying innocent blood. [Mt. xxvii, 4]

24. At the same time Moses was born, and he was handsome in the presence of God. [Acts vii, 20]

25. Then Jesus gave to his apostles power over evil spirits.

26. For I also (am) a man under authority. [Mt. viii, 9]

27. And looking he was saying: "I see men, just as though I see trees walking. [Mk. viii, 24]

28. And behold, nothing worthy of death has been done by the Nazarene.

29. Go away from me, because I am a man (who is) a sinner, Lord. [Lk. v, 8]

30. And seeing the star they rejoiced very much with great joy. [Mt. ii, 10]

31. Lamb of God, you who take away the sins of the world, have mercy on us.

II.   1. Fidēs nostra firmētur cōtīdiē!

   2. Ōrēmus Dominum dōnāre nōbīs pācem.

   3. Apostolus miser trādere Jēsūm ausus est.

   4. Gaudeāmus quoniam Dominus nōbīs misertus est.

   5. Quārē opus erat Jōannī Jēsūm baptizāre?
      Quārē Jēsūs Jōannī baptizandus erat?

Unit 21

Drills

I. a. misereātur: 3rd sg. present deponent subjunctive ("may he/she have pity")

    misereantur: 3rd pl. present deponent subjunctive ("may they have pity")

    miserētur: 3rd sg. present deponent indicative ("he/she has pity")

    miserentur: 3rd pl. present deponent indicative ("they have pity")

b. trādant: 3rd pl. present active subjunctive ("may they hand over")

    trādat: 3rd sg. present active subjunctive ("may he/she/it hand over")

    trādunt: 3rd pl. present active indicative ("they [are] hand[ing] over")

    trādit: 3rd sg. present active indicative ("he/she/it hands / is handing over")

c. trādent: 3rd pl. future active indicative ("they will hand over")

    trādet: 3rd sg. future active indicative ("he/she/it will hand over")

d. trādunt: 3rd pl. present active indicative ("they [are] hand[ing] over")

    trādit: 3rd sg. present active indicative ("he/she/it hands / is handing over")

83

e. dēleātur: 3rd sg. present passive subjunctive ("may he/she/it be destroyed")

dēleantur: 3rd pl. present passive subjunctive ("may they be destroyed")

dēlētur: 3rd sg. present passive indicative ("he/she/it is [being] destroyed")

dēlentur: 3rd pl. present passive indicative ("they are [being] destroyed")

f. habeāmus: 1st pl. present active subjunctive ("may we have")

habeam: 1st sg. present active subjunctive ("may I have")

habēmus: 1st pl. present active indicative ("we have")

habeō: 1st sg. present active indicative ("I have")

g. agāmus: 1st pl. present active subjunctive ("may we do")

agam: 1st sg. present active subjunctive ("may I do")

agimus: 1st pl present active indicative ("we [are] do[ing]")

agō: 1st sg. present active indicative ("I [am] do[ing]")

h. jungāminī: 2nd pl. present passive subjunctive ("may you be joined")

jungāris, jungāre: 2nd sg. present passive subjunctive ("may you be joined")

jungiminī: 2nd pl. present passive indicative ("you are [being] joined")

jungeris, jungere: 2nd sg. present passive indicative ("you are [being] joined")

i. sciātis: 2nd pl. present active subjunctive ("may you know")

sciās: 2nd sg. present active subjunctive ("may you know")

scītis: 2nd pl. present active indicative ("you know")

scīs: 2nd sg. present active indicative ("you know")

j. veniās: 2nd sg. present active subjunctive ("may you come")

veniātis: 2nd pl. present active subjunctive ("may you come")

venīs: 2nd sg. present active indicative ("you come / are coming")

venītis: 2nd pl. present active indicative ("you come / are coming")

k. veniēs: 2nd sg. future active indicative ("you will come / will be coming")

veniētis: 2nd pl. future active indicative ("you will come / will be coming")

l. dīcātur: 3rd sg. present passive subjunctive ("may he/she/it be said")

dīcantur: 3rd pl. present passive subjunctive ("may they be said")

dīcitur: 3rd sg. present passive indicative ("he/she/it is [being] said")

dīcuntur: 3rd pl. present passive indicative ("they are [being] said")

m. nāscāmur: 1st pl. present deponent subjunctive ("may we be born")

nāscar: 1st sg. present deponent subjunctive ("may I be born")

nāscimur: 1st pl. present deponent indicative ("we are [being] born")

nāscor: 1st sg. present deponent indicative ("I am [being] born")

n. audiant: 3rd pl. present active subjunctive ("may they hear")

audiat: 3rd sg. present active subjunctive ("may he/she/it hear")

audiunt: 3rd pl. present active indicative ("they [are] hear[ing]")

audit: 3rd sg. present active indicative ("he/she/it hears / is hearing")

o. tollās: 2nd sg. present active subjunctive ("may you take away")

tollātis: 2nd pl. present active subjunctive ("may you take away")

tollis: 2nd sg. present active indicative ("you take away / are taking away")

tollitis: 2nd pl. present active indicative ("you take away / are taking away")

II. 1. *Simple present:* If we send Paul to Rome, he sees Peter.

2. *Future more vivid:* If we (will) send Paul to Rome, he will see Peter.

3. *Future more vivid:* If we send / will have sent Paul to Rome, he will see Peter.

4. *Future less vivid:* If we should send Paul to Rome, he would see Peter.

5. *Simple past:* If we did not send Paul, he did not go to Rome.

6. *Future more vivid:* If the boys do not work / will not have worked, they will not eat supper.

Exercises

I.   1. If therefore the Son frees you, you will be truly free. [Jn. viii, 36]

2. If *I* produce testimony about myself, my testimoney is not true. [Jn. v, 31]

3. May almighty God bless you, the Father and the Son and the Holy Spirit.

4. For God said: "Honor (your) father and mother" and: "He who curses (his) father or mother, let him die by death." [Mt. xv, 4]

5. But this crowd, which does not know the law, they are cursed! [Jn. vii, 49]

6. You know neither me nor my Father. [Jn. viii, 19]

7. And stretching out (his) hand, he touched him. [Mt. viii, 3]

8. And Jesus, filled with the Holy Spirit, returned from the Jordan and was led by the Spirit in the desert. [Lk. iv, 1]

9. For John came neither eating nor drinking. [Mt. xi, 18]

10. What therefore God has joined, let man not separate. [Mt. xix, 6]

11. May the body of our Lord Jesus Christ guard your soul into eternal life.

12. For in the spirit by faith we look for the hope of righteousness. [Gal. v, 5]

13. If I speak the truth, why do you not believe me? [Jn. viii, 46]

14. Now let the angelic multitude of heaven rejoice: let the divine mysteries rejoice: and for the victory of so great a King let the saving trumpet resound.

15. Brothers, let us acknowledge our sins.

16. May almighty God have mercy on us, and, with our sins forgiven, may he lead us to eternal life.

17. And I look for the resurrection of the dead, and the life of the age about to come.

18. Afterwards, if it should be considered, the second reading is read.

19. May the Lord accept the sacrifice from your hands to the praise and glory of his own name.

20. Let us give thanks to the Lord our God.
    It is worthy and just (to do so).

21. Are you (the one) who is going to come? [Mt. xi, 3]

22. Amen, amen I say to you: unless you eat the flesh of the Son of man and drink his blood, you will not have life in you at all. [Jn. vi, 53]

23. I therefore have said to you that you will die in your sins, for if you do not believe that I am (he), you will die in your sins. [Jn. viii, 24]

24. Mary wept and embraced (her) Son.

25. Let us try to pray to the Lord with contrite heart.

26. Jesus suffered and was buried, and he arose on the third day, according to the Scriptures.

27. The woman consoled the old man, who was bewailing the loss of (his) son.

28. Let us rejoice together with the holy heaven-dwellers, who have the crown of glory.

29. Blessed (are those) who know the presence of the Lord and walk in his paths.

30. Jesus, touched by the weeping of the four women, went back and consoled them.

31. The old shepherd, leading seven sheep, was walking along to the mountain.

32. With our needs foreknown by the Lord, let us be made a people of constant devotion.

33. May the priest perform the rites by which our substance is nourished. Nor may they cease to nourish (us)!

II.   1. Sī Petrus Rōmam regressus erit, invenietne frātrēs fidēlēs
           doctrīnīs Jēsū?

        2. Jēsūs praenōvit quia moritūrus erat.

        3. Mortuī mortuōs sepeliant!

        4. Utinam omnēs pācem Chrīstī cognōscant!

        5. Cōnēmur cōnsōlārī / cōnsōlāre mulierem lacrimantem?

Readings

1.   The Gloria.

       Glory in the highest to God and on earth peace to men of good will.
       We praise you, we bless you, we adore you, we glorify you, we give
       thanks to you because of your great glory, Lord God, heavenly King,
       God the Father almighty. Lord only begotten Son, Jesus Christ, Lord
       God, Lamb of God, Son of the Father, you who take away the sins
       of the world, have mercy on us; you who take away the sins of the
       world, receive our prayer. You who sit at the right hand of the Father,
       have mercy on us. Because you alone (are) the Holy One, you alone
       (are) the Lord, you alone (are) the Most High, Jesus Christ, with the
       Holy Spirit: in the glory of God the Father. Amen.

2.   A reading of the holy Gospel according to Mark i, 40–42. (Jesus cures
       a leper.) And a leprous (man) comes to him, beseeching him and
       kneeling down and saying to him: "If you will (it), you are able to
       cleanse me." And having pity, stretching out his hand he touched him
       and said to him: "I do will (it), be cleansed!"; and immediately the
       leprosy departed from him, and he was cleansed.

Unit 22

Drills

I. 1. The man cries out in order that he may be heard.

    2. The man cried out in order that he might be heard.

    3. The man has cried out in order that he may be heard.

    4. The servant enters the house in order that he may prepare supper.

    5. The servant had left the house in order that he might not be called by the master.

    6. Jesus sent the apostles to preach the Gospel.

    7. Do we have enough food to eat?

    8. John came to produce testimony about Jesus.

II. 1. Let us beseech Mary to pray for us.

    2. Let us pray God to forgive us our debts.

    3. We pray God that he forgive us our debts.

    4. Paul warned the brothers that they (should) keep the commandments.

    5. Jesus told the apostles to preach the Gospel.

    6. Jesus bade the apostles to preach the Gospel.

7. Let us ask God that he regard us.

8. We ask God to regard us.

9. We (have) asked the Father for our daily bread.

10. The boy asked the teacher for a book.

11. The priests had warned the Romans not to destroy the temple.

Exercises

I.   1. For Christ did not send me to baptize but to preach the Gospel. [I Cor. i, 17]

2. The weeping of the women moved Jesus to tears and concern.

3. Therefore every one who acknowledges me in the presence of men, I also will acknowledge him in the presence of my Father, who is in heaven. [Mt. x, 32]

4. Let him take up the cross and follow me.

5. I have not come to call the just but (to call) sinners. [Mk. ii, 17]

6. A common or unclean (thing) has never entered into my mouth. [Acts xi, 8]

7. And immediately then the brothers sent Paul away, in order that he might go all the way to the sea. [Acts xvii, 14]

8. I confess to you, Father, Lord of heaven and of earth. [Mt. xi, 25]

9. But we have received not the spirit of the world, but the Spirit, who is from God, in order that we may know (the things) which have been given to us by God. [I Cor. ii, 12]

10. Therefore glorify God in your body. [I Cor. vi, 20]

11. For I am the least of the apostles, who am not worthy to be called an apostle, because I have persecuted the church of God. [I Cor. xv, 9]

12. For the Jews do not have dealings with the Samaritans. [Jn. iv, 9]

13. The woman answered and said to him: "I do not have a husband." [Jn. iv, 17]

14. I am he, I who speak with you. [Jn. iv, 26]

15. I have food to eat which you do not know about. [Jn. iv, 32]

16. But many of the Samaritans from that city believed in him because of the word of the woman testifying: "He told me all things, whatever I have done." [Jn. iv, 39]

17. Through the intercession of Mary and of all the saints, let us ask the Father that he deign to look upon us.

18. The Father, mindful of us, sent (his) Son to free us from our sins.

19. If we should judge, we would be judged.

20. Let us profess our faith in Christ Jesus.

21. Confessing (their) faults, they asked God for forgiveness.

22. The apostles were asking Jesus about the mercy of the Father.

23. Jesus did not scorn the woman but spoke to (her).

24. John came first in order that a greater (one) might follow.

25. And Jesus was preaching daily in the temple, in order that he might do the will of the Father.

26. The crown of thorns (is) a crown of glory.

27. Then our bishop read the introit of the Mass of the day.

28. The brothers praise the Lord with joyful songs.

29. For the greater glory of God.

30. Let us bid the Lord to save us so that we may not be lost.

31. Let us ask Jesus that the light of his serene countenance appear to us.

II.   1. Petrus, persequēns Jēsūm, (eum) ōrantem invēnit.

2. Jēsūs exierat ut ōrāret.

3. Petrus jussit Dominum ad cīvitātem regredī.

4. Dominus autem petīvit ā Petrō ut ad proximam cīvitātem īret.

Readings

1.   The Confiteor (old style).

I confess to almighty God, to blessed Mary ever Virgin, to blessed Michael the Archangel, to blessed John the Baptist, to the holy Apostles Peter and Paul, to all the Saints, and to you, brothers: that I have sinned greatly in thought, in word, and in deed; through my fault, through my fault, though my most grievous fault. Therefore I beseech blessed Mary ever Virgin, blessed Michael the Archangel, blessed John the Baptist, the holy Apostles Peter and Paul, all the Saints, and you, brothers, to pray for me to the Lord our God.

2.   A reading of the holy Gospel according to John i, 1–9.

In the beginning was the Word, and the Word was with God, and the Word was God. This (Word) was in the beginning with God. All things were made through him, and without him was made nothing which has been made; in him was life, and the life was the light of men, and the light shines in the darkness, and the darkness has not overcome it. There was a man sent by God, whose name was John; he came for testimony, in order that he might present testimony concerning the light, in order that all might believe through him. He was not the light, but (he came) in order that he might present testimony concerning the light. The true light, which enlightens every man, was coming into the world.

Unit 23

Drills

I. 1. hujus spīnae: genitive singular ("of this thorn")
       hārum spīnārum: genitive plural ("of these thorns")

    2. illārum cūrārum: genitive plural ("of those cares")
       illīus cūrae: genitive singular ("of that care")

    3. huic puerō: dative singular ("for/to this boy")
       hīs puerīs: dative plural ("for/to these boys")

    4. hīs mulieribus: dative plural ("for/to these women")
       huic mulierī: dative singular ("for/to this woman")

       hīs mulieribus: ablative plural ("from/with/in/by these women")
       hāc muliere: ablative singular ("from/with/in/by this woman")

    5. illī rēgī: dative singular ("for/to that king")
       illīs rēgibus: dative plural ("for/to those kings")

    6. illī rēgēs: nominative plural ("those kings")
       ille rēx: nominative singular ("that king")

    7. hunc virum: accusative singular ("this man")
       hōs virōs: accusative plural ("these men")

    8. hoc vitium: nominative/accusative singular ("this fault")
       haec vitia: nominative/accusative plural ("these faults")

    9. illam cīvitātem: accusative singular ("that city")
       illās cīvitātēs: accusative plural ("those cities")

93

10. hōc modō: ablative singular ("from/with/in/by this manner")
    hīs modīs: ablative plural ("from/with/in/by these manners")

11. hāc corōnā: ablative singular ("from/with/in/by this crown")
    hīs corōnīs: ablative plural ("from/with/in/by these crowns")

12. illīus patris: genitive singular ("of that father")
    illōrum patrum: genitive plural ("of those fathers")

13. illud opus: nominative/accusative singular ("that work")
    illa opera: nominative/accusative plural ("those works")

14. haec scelera: nominative/accusative plural ("these crimes")
    hoc scelus: nominative/accusative singular ("this crime")

15. huic memoriae: dative singular ("for/to this memory")
    hīs memoriīs: dative plural ("for/to these memories")

16. haec māter: nominative singular ("this mother")
    hae mātrēs: nominative plural ("these mothers")

17. hī caelicolae: nominative plural ("these heaven-dwellers")
    hic caelicola: nominative singular ("this heaven-dweller")

18. illīs arboribus: dative plural ("for/to those trees")
    illī arborī: dative singular ("for/to that tree")

    illīs arboribus: ablative plural ("from/with/in/by those trees")
    illā arbore: ablative singular ("from/with/in/by that tree")

19. ille peccātor: nominative singular ("that sinner")
    illī peccātōrēs: nominative plural ("those sinners")

20. haec nox: nominative singular ("this night")
    hae noctēs: nominative plural ("these nights")

II. 1. Mary is so sad, that she is not able to recognize Jesus.

     2. The man was so full of faith, that he was cured.

     3. Jesus so spoke, that the woman called him Lord.

     4. He so prays, that God hears him.

     5. They so suffered, that the Lord had pity on them.

III.　1.　He is (the sort) who sings well.

　　　2.　Those women were (the sort) who always wept.

　　　3.　They are (the sort) unworthy to approach the altar of God.

　　　4.　You know the (sort of) prayer which glorifies the Lord.

　　　5.　Are they (the sort) who break bread with you?

　　　6.　They are (the sort) who do not believe in Jesus.

Exercises

I.　1.　Glory (be) to the Father, and to the Son, and to the Holy Spirit. As it was in the beginning, and now, and always, and forever. Amen.

　　2.　Do this in my remembrance. [Lk. xxii, 19]

　　3.　He will teach us all things. [Jn. xiv, 26]

　　4.　And we know that all things work together toward the good for (those) loving God, who have been called according to (his) decree. [Rom. viii, 28]

　　5.　He was (the sort) who wished to betray Jesus.

　　6.　Do you see that faith was working together with his works? [James ii, 22]

　　7.　Be faithful all the way to death, and I will give you the crown of life. [Rev. ii, 10]

　　8.　And when you pray you will not be like the hypocrites, who love to pray standing in the synagogues and at the street corners, in order that they may be seen by men. [Mt. vi, 5]

　　9.　I am the true vine. [Jn. xv, 1]

　　10.　Thus passes away the glory of the world.

　　11.　This is the night about which it was written: And the night will be made to shine like the day: And the night (is) my light in my delights.

12. This night returns innocence to the fallen and joy to the saddened.

13. And the boy was healed at that hour. [Mt. viii, 13]

14. Behold, I will make them come and worship before your feet and know that I have loved you. [Rev. iii, 9]

15. For God so loved the world, that he gave his only begotten Son, in order that every one who believes in him may not perish, but may have life eternal. [Jn. iii, 16]

16. If we should confess our sins, he is (so) faithful and just, that he would forgive us (our) sins. [I Jn. i, 9]

17. But the Son of man does not have (a place) where he may recline (his) head. [Mt. viii, 20]

18. And with him having been seen / when he was seen, they asked that he pass away from their boundaries. [Mt. viii, 34] [Review the ablative absolute in Collins, p. 104.]

19. Unless we should be doers of the word, we would not be saved.

20. You are a priest forever according to the order of Melchisedech. [Heb. v, 6]

21. Those women so protected the little ones, that they all called them good mothers / they called them all good mothers..

22. But the master, taking pity on his servant, released him and forgave him his debt. [Mt. xviii, 27]

23. Unless you perform good works, you will not obtain the kingdom of heaven.

24. My kingdom is not of this world. [Jn. xviii, 36]

25. For who knows the mind of the Lord? [I Cor. ii, 16]

26. So also they have now not believed because of your mercy [i.e., the mercy obtained by you Gentiles from God], in order that even they may now obtain mercy. [Rom. xi, 31]

27. He who sees me sees him who has sent me. [Jn. xii, 45]

28. I will give you all these things, if falling down you worship me. [Mt. iv, 9]

29. For the Father also seeks such ones who worship him. [Jn. iv, 23]

30. For wicked thoughts go out from the heart. [Mt. xv, 19]

31. May the peace of the Lord be always with you.

32. Depart from me, you who perform wickedness. [Mt. vii, 23]

33. Of what kind and how great are the works of the Lord!

34. May the saving trumpet resound for the victory of so great a King!

35. In the sixth hour they returned to the city, where the king, sitting in judgment, might grant them favor.

II. 1. Tanta est cūra Deī prō nōbīs, ut semper gaudēre possīmus.

  2. Sunt quī ōrent ut ā virīs laudentur.

  3. Suntne quī sint tam miserī ut credere in Chrīstō nōn possint?

  4. Puerī in vītibus assiduā cum cūrā sīc cooperātī sunt, ut sedēre et cēnāre nōn possent.

[Note: Review Collins, p. 183, for the *imperfect* subjunctive of **possum**.]

Readings

1. The Nicene Creed.

    I believe in one God, Father almighty, maker of heaven and of earth, of all things visible and invisible. And in one Lord Jesus Christ, only begotten Son of God, and born from the Father before all ages. God from God, light from light, true God from true God, begotten, not made, consubstantial with the Father: through whom all things were made. Who for the sake of us men and for the sake of our salvation came down from heaven. He was made incarnate from the Holy Spirit out of the Virgin Mary, and he became man. He was also crucified for us under Pontius Pilate; he suffered and was buried, and arose on the third day, according to the Scriptures, and ascended into heaven, (and) sits at the right hand of the Father. And he is going to come again in glory to judge the living and the dead, and of his kingdom there will not be an end. And (I believe) in the Holy Spirit, Lord and life-maker, who proceeds from the Father and the Son. Who together with the Father and the Son is worshipped and glorified; who has spoken through the prophets. And (I believe in) one holy, catholic and apostolic Church. I confess one baptism for the forgiveness of sins. And I look for the resurrection of the dead, and the life of the world to come.

2.   A reading of the holy Gospel according to John i, 10–13.

He was in the world,
and the world was made through him,
and the world did not know him.
Into his own he came,
and his own did not accept him.
But as many as did accept him,
he gave to them the power to become sons of God,
to these who believe in his name, who are born not from blood nor
from the will of the flesh nor from the will of man, but from God.

Unit 24

Drills

I.   1. If a bad shepherd were watching the sheep, they would be lost.

     2. If the king were dying, (his) family would return.

     3. If he were not an apostle, he would not betray Jesus.

     4. If you believed in Christ, you would now rejoice.

     5. The priest would now perform the rite, if he were here.

II.   1. To finish a prayer the people say: Amen.

     2. We get to know many things by reading.

     3. We get to know many things by reading books.

     4. He himself gave the apostles the power of healing.

     5. Jesus went out to call the apostles.

     6. Instead of cursing the man Jesus blessed him.

     7. Instead of cursing the man Jesus blessed him.

     8. The wicked (men) spoke about killing Jesus.

     9. They themselves entered into the upper room to eat the Pasch.

    10. The kings rejoiced at seeing the star.

    11. By going into the desert John was able to satisfy (his) desire to baptize the people.

Exercises

I. 1. Blessed (are) the meek, because they will possess the earth. [Mt. v, 4]

2. And he instructed the crowd to sit on the ground.

3. But in order that you may know that the Son of man has power on earth to forgive sins . . . : I say to you: Arise, take your cot and go into your house. [Mk. ii, 10–11]

4. And with a hymn having been sung, they went out to the mount of Olivet. [Mt. xxvi, 30]

5. On that day you will ask in my name, and I do not say to you that I will ask the Father about you; for the Father himself loves you, because you have loved me and have believed that I came from God. I came from the Father and I have come into the world; again I am leaving the world and am going to the Father. [Jn. xvi, 26–28]

6. But see yourselves. [Mk. xiii, 9]

7. Make yourself safe (by) descending from the cross. [Mk. xv, 30]

8. O Lord, Creator Spirit, kindle in our hearts the fire of your love.

9. The prophets have prophesied to illuminate the mind of God.

10. With Jesus having been buried, the five women were mourning greatly.

11. Truly this man was the Son of God. [Mk. xv, 39]

12. For to this you have been called, because Christ also suffered for you, leaving you an example, in order that you may follow his footsteps. [I Pet. ii, 21]

13. A few, that is, eight souls, were saved through water. [I Pet. iii, 20]

14. But, to the extent that you share in the sufferings of Christ, rejoice, in order that you may rejoice also in the revelation of his glory, exulting. [I Pet. iv, 13]

15. To him (is) the power forever and ever. Amen. [I Pet. v, 11]

16. It is enough, the hour has come: behold, the Son of man is betrayed into the hands of sinners. Rise, let us go; behold, the one who betrays me is near. [Mk. xiv, 41–42]

17. The spirit indeed (is) ready, but the flesh indeed (is) weak. [Mk. xiv, 38]

18. And kneeling they worshipped him. [Mk. xv, 19]

19. And because of this I ask you to take food, for this is for your health. [Acts xxvii, 34]

20. Let us go up to Bethlehem and let us see this word, which has been done, which the Lord shows to us. [Lk. ii, 15]

21. My food is that I do the will of him who sent me, and that I complete his work. [Jn. iv, 34]

22. He is not here, for he has arisen, as He said. Come, see the place where he was buried. [Mt. xxviii, 6]

23. For many are called, but indeed few chosen. [Mt. xxii, 14]

24. All things therefore, whatsoever you wish that men do to you, so also you do to them; for this is the Law and the Prophets. [Mt. vii, 12]

25. And he went out again to the sea; and all the crowd came to him, and he taught them. [Mk. ii, 13]

26. The first man (was) from the earth earthly, the second man (was) from heaven. As (was) the earthly (man), so also (are) the earthly, and as (is) the heavenly (man) so (are) the heavenly; and just as we have carried the image of the earthly (one), we will also carry the image of the heavenly (one). [I Cor. xv, 47–49]

27. But may the God of hope fill you with every joy and peace in believing. [Rom. xv, 13]

28. From him and through him and in him (are) all things. To him glory forever. Amen. [Rom. xi, 36]

29. And one of them will not fall / not one of them will fall on the ground without your Father. [Mt. x, 29]

30. You have sent to John, and he has produced testimony to the truth; but I do not receive testimony from man, but I say this in order that you may be saved. [Jn. v, 33–34]

31. Blessed (are those) with clean heart, because they will see God. [Mt. v, 8]

32. Behold, I see the heavens opened and the Son of man standing at the right hand of God. [Acts vii, 56]

33. Neither me do you know nor my Father; if you knew me, perhaps you would also know my Father. [Jn. viii, 19]

34. But I ask you, permit me to speak to the people. [Acts xxi, 39]

35. You are the light of the world. [Mt. v, 14]

36. For if you believed in Moses, you would perhaps also believe in me. [Jn. v, 46]

37. For there were many who were coming and going, and they did not have space to eat. [Mk. vi, 31]

38. At once therefore I sent for you, and you did well by coming. [Acts x, 33]

39. For we ourselves have heard and we know that this (man) is truly the Savior of the world! [Jn. iv, 42]

40. He who has ears [for hearing], let him hear. [Mt. xiii, 9]

41. You shall love your neighbor as yourself. [Mt. xxii, 39]

42. If you loved me, you would rejoice that I go to the Father, because the Father is greater than I. [Jn. xiv, 28]

43. Though the mystery of this water and wine, may we be made partakers of his divinity.

44. May this mingling of the Body and Blood of our Lord Jesus Christ be (a way) into eternal life for us receiving (it).

45. As soon as the eighty soldiers went into the city, the women cried aloud about their sins.

II. 1. Jēsūs sēdit ad pānem frangendum cum apostolīs.

2. Sī fidem nostram in Dominō ponerēmus, adventum ejus laetē exspectārēmus.

3. Simulac Jēsūs in cīvitātem advēnit, vēnit ad templum docendī causā.

4. Subeundō in montem et simul eum persequendō, Petrus Jēsūm ipsum invenīre poterat.

Readingѕ

1. Preface for the Nativity.

It is truly worthy and just, fair and saving, for us always and every-where to give thanks to you: holy Lord, Father almighty, eternal God: Because through the mystery of the incarnate Word, the new light of your glory has shone on the eyes of our mind: so that, until we get to know God visibly, through this (one) we may be taken up into (his) invisible love. And therefore with the Angels and Archangels, with the Thrones and Dominions, and with all the soldiery of the heavenly army, we sing a hymn to your glory, saying without end: Holy, holy, holy . . .

2. A reading of the holy Gospel according to John i, 14–18.

And the Word was made flesh
and dwelt among us,
and we saw his glory,
the glory as of the Only-begotten from the Father,
full of grace and of truth.
John produces testimony about him and cries out saying: "This was
    (the one about) whom I said: He who is going to come after me,
    he was made before me, because he was before me."
And from his fullness we have all received,
and grace for grace;
because the law was given through Moses, (but) grace and truth was
    made through Jesus Christ. No one has ever seen God; the only
    begotten God, who is in the bosom of the Father, he himself has
    explained (this).

Unit 25

Drills

I. 1. If the deacon had come to the hall, we would have seen him.

2. If you had read the book, you would have known this.

3. If the man had not been healed, he would have died.

4. The sheep would have been lost, if the shepherd had not watched them.

5. If you had helped us, we would now be doing well.

II. 1. They feared that Peter had seen Paul.

2. I feared that Peter did not see (was not going to see) Paul.

3. Paul was afraid that they had not heard about Jesus.

4. The people are afraid that they are not going to have enough food.

5. Are you not afraid that the Roman soldiers are going to betray you?

Exercises

I. 1. O surely necessary sin of Adam, which was detroyed by the death of Christ!

2. Through him, and with him, and in him, (there) is to you God the Father almighty in the unity of the Holy Spirit all honor and glory forever and ever. Amen.

3. And abandoning him they all fled. [Mk. xiv, 50]

4. It was good for him, if that man had not been born. [Mt. xxvi, 24]

5. Lord, if you had been here, my brother would not have died! [Jn. xi, 32]

6. For if a law had been given which was able to give life, truly justice would be from the law. [Gal. iii, 21]

7. The prophet is not without honor, except in his own country and his own home. [Mt. xiii, 57]

8. Hail, full of grace, the Lord (is) with you [blessed (are) you among women]. [Lk. i, 28]

9. Look also at our devout Emperor!

10. The Jews were afraid that the disciples of Jesus would take away his body.

11. The crowd demanded that Jesus be condemned to death.

12. If this (man) were not an evil-doer, we would not have handed him over to you. [Jn. xviii, 30]

13. Jesus answered and said to her: "If you knew the gift of God and who it is who says to you, 'Give to me to drink,' you perhaps would have asked him and he would have given you living water." [Jn. iv, 10]

14. Then all the disciples, with him having been abandoned, fled. [Mt. xxvi, 56]

15. For even if there are those who are said (to be) gods either in heaven or on earth, if indeed there are many gods and many lords, to us nevertheless (there is) one God the Father, from whom (are) all things and we (are) in him, and (there is) one Lord Jesus Christ, through whom (are) all things and we (are/exist) through him. [I Cor. viii, 5–6]

16. You are from (your) father the Devil and you wish to do the desires of your father. [Jn. viii, 44]

17. For whether we live, we live in the Lord, or whether we die, we die in the Lord. Therefore, whether we live or die, we are the Lord's. [Rom. xiv, 8]

18. For if they had known, they would never have crucified the Lord of glory. [I Cor. ii, 8]

19. Outside the city the daughters of Jerusalem, full of sorrow, were weeping at the cross of Jesus.

20. Blessed (are) the poor in spirit, because theirs is the kingdom of heaven. [Mt. v, 3]

21. Jesus rose, just as he foretold, alleluia.

22. May the Lord receive our offering with kindness.

23. Hail, Michael the Archangel! May you always defend us from the devil.

24. Peter ran up to Jesus (as he was) disputing with the Jews.

25. Standing around the body of Jesus, the women were weeping with an outpouring of tears, crying out: "Why has the Lord died? Would that he were still living!"

26. The rich (man) was perpetually afraid that (his) yearly prayer would not be enough.

II. 1. Utinam mīlitēs Rōmānī cīvitātem dēfendisset!

2. Dēprecātus est diāconus Patrem ut nōs veniā respiceret?

3. Timuistīne ut sacerdōs populō succursūrus esset?

4. Nisi Petrus cīvitātem fūgisset, Rōmānīs trāditus esset.

5. Fīlia pauperis mortua esset nisi Jēsūs ad domum advēnisset et eam sānāvisset.

6. Puer salvus adhūc esset nisi malīs occurrisset.

Readings

1. The Salve Regina (Hermann Contractus, c. 1054).

    Hail, Queen, Mother of mercy, our life, sweetness, and hope, hail. To you we banished children of Eve cry out. To you we sigh, groaning and weeping in this valley of tears. Come, therefore, our advocate, turn those merciful eyes of yours toward us. And after this exile show us Jesus the blessed fruit of your womb. O merciful, O tender, O sweet Virgin Mary.

    V. Pray for us, holy Mother of God.

    R. That we may be made worthy of the promises of Christ.

2. A reading of the holy Gospel according to Luke i, 26–28.

    The Annunciation.

    But in the sixth month the angel Gabriel was sent by God into a city of Galilee, whose name (was) Nazareth, to a virgin engaged to a man, whose name was Joseph from the house of David, and the name of the virgin (was) Mary. And having come in, the angel said to her: "Hail, full of grace, the Lord (is) with you" [blessed (are) you among women].

Unit 26

Drills

I.   1. Do you know if Paul came?

    2. He asked why the women were mourning.

    3. Peter knew where Jesus had taught.

    4. The disciple was asking when Paul was killed by the Romans.

    5. Did you hear if Paul will see Peter?

II. 1. If anyone wishes to be saved, let him follow me.

    2. If someone does not aid this wretch, he will surely die.

    3. By whom was the book written? By John perhaps?

    4. With whom was Peter dining?

    5. With what words were the apostles taught by Jesus?

    6. What feast-days do you celebrate?

    7. What did you see in the field?

    8. Why did he not take the bread?

    9. To whom will they give the crown?

    10. Whom were they calling King of the Jews?

11. Whose is the kingdom of heaven?

12. Who is my mother? Who are my brothers?

Exercises

I. 1. And he asked who he was and what he had done. [Acts xxi, 33]

2. Whom do you wish (that) I release to you: Barabbas or Jesus, who is called Christ? [Mt. xxvii, 17]

3. Was Paul crucified for you, or were you baptized in the name of Paul? [I Cor. i, 13]

4. If I said earthy things to you, and you do not believe, how will you believe if I say heavenly things to you? [Jn. iii, 12]

5. But you have a custom that I release one to you on the Passover; do you wish therefore that I release to you the king of the Jews? [Jn. xviii, 39]

6. Who will separate us from the love of Christ? [Rom. viii, 35]

7. If anyone seems to be a prophet or spiritual, let him acknowledge that what I am writing to you is a command of the Lord. [I Cor. xiv, 37]

8. O man, but who are you who respond to God? [Rom. ix, 20]

9. But I praise you because in all respects you are mindful of me. [I Cor. xi, 2]

10. And having gone out he went according to (his) custom to the Mount of Olives. [Lk. xxii, 39]

11. For I say to you: I shall not eat it, until it is fulfilled in the kingdom of God. [Lk. xxii, 16]

12. May you deign to strengthen in faith and love your Church, a pilgrim on earth, together with your servant our Pope John Paul and with our Bishop N., with the episcopal order and all the clergy and all the people of your acquisition.

13. With the morning star having risen, a new life has been breathed into us who believe in the teaching of the resurrection. [Review Collins p. 104 on the ablative absolute and p. 127 on translating the present participle.]

14. How therefore were your eyes opened? [Jn. ix, 10]

15. Can it be that you do not know that your body is a temple of the Holy Spirit, who is in you, whom you have from God, and you are not your own? [I Cor. vi, 19]

16. Moses gave you the law, did he not? [Jn. vii, 19]

17. But this I say according to concession, not according to command. [I Cor. vii, 6]

18. Can it be that you do not know that the saints will judge regarding the world? [I Cor. vi, 2]

19. Why do you question me? Question those who have heard what I have said to them; behold, they know what *I* have said. [Jn. xviii, 21]

20. And if anyone says to you: "Why are you doing this?" say: "It is needful to the Lord." [Mk. xi, 3]

21. But answering, Judas, who betrayed him, said: "I am not he, am I, Rabbi?" [Mt. xxvi, 25]

22. And they were watching him, (to see) if he might heal that (man) on the Sabbath. [Mk. iii, 2]

23. And forgive us our debts, as we also forgive our debtors. [Mt. vi, 12]

24. While they waited for the teacher Jesus, the disciples, standing strong in (their) faith, were praying in the house. [Review the note on translating the present tense in **dum** clauses in Collins, p. 107.]

25. Teacher, what good may I do, that I may have eternal life? [Mt. xix, 16]

26. Saint Peter, our patron, lead to triumph the martyrs working for the Lord.

27. For (it is) clear that our Lord sprang up from Judah. [Heb. vii, 14]

28. (As) pilgrims on earth we make the journey to the kingdom of heaven.

29. Therefore, brothers, we are debtors, not to the flesh in order that we may live according to the flesh. [Rom. viii, 12]

30. What does it avail me? If the dead do not rise, *let us eat and let us drink, for tomorrow we will die.* [I Cor. xv, 32]

31. How is this (man) able to give us his own flesh to eat? [Jn. vi, 52]

32. What therefore will we say to these things? If God (is) for us, who (is) against us? [Rom. viii, 31]

33. But also if you suffer anything for the sake of justice, (you are) blessed! [I Pet. iii, 14]

34. A mystery of faith: we announce your death , Lord, and we confess your resurrection, until you come.

35. But how he now sees we do not know, or who has opened his eyes we do not know. [Jn. ix, 21]

36. Who can give back that which has been lost?

37. And behold, they cried out saying: "What (is there) to us and to you [i.e., what have you to do with us], Son of God?" [Mt. viii, 29]

38. For the poor you always have with you, but me you do not always have. [Mt. xxvi, 11]

II. 1. Scīs quandō Jēsūs vītam spīrāverit in filiam mīlitis Rōmānī?

2. Dum labōrāmus, ōrāmus.

3. Prō quibus prīmī martyrēs mortuī sunt / exspīrāvērunt?

4. Puer rogat doctōrem quārē martyr nōn sepultus sit secundum cōnsuētūdinem Jūdaeōrum.

5. a) Scripsitne Jōannēs hunc librum?
   b) Nōnne Jōannēs hunc librum scripsit?
   c) Numquid Jōannēs hunc librum scripsit?

Readings

1.   The Last Supper, as understood by Paul, I Cor. xi, 23–26.

   For I received from the Lord what I also handed down to you, that the Lord Jesus, on the night on which he was betrayed, took bread and giving thanks broke (it) and said: *"This is my body, which is for you; do this in my commemoration"*; in the same way the cup, after they dined, saying: *"This cup is the new covenant in my blood; do this, as often as you drink (it), in my commemoration."* For as often as you eat this bread and drink the cup, you proclaim the Lord's death until he comes.

2.   Hail, queen of heaven,
   hail, mistress of angels,
   hail, source, hail, gate,
   from whom the light has risen in the world:
   rejoice, glorious virgin,
   beautiful above all,
   hail, O very fitting,
   and for us beseech Christ.

Unit 27

Drills

I. 1. This Levite is the most faithful of all.

2. Who is more worthy than you?

3. Dearest brothers, what is more wonderful than the resurrection of Jesus?

4. Glory to God in the highest.

5. That church was nearest to the sea.

6. On the last day we will all rise up.

7. We were created a little less than the angels.

8. Who has greater love than this?

9. More men were coming together into the temple.

10. The elders were watching Jesus.

11. These are much worse than those.

12. Give this to the most wretched among you.

13. I am the Alpha and the Omega, the first and the last, the beginning and the end. [Rev. xxii, 13]

Exercises

I.   1. And coming into his own country, he was teaching them in their synogogue, so that they were amazed and said: "From where (come) this wisdom and (these) miracles to this (man)?" [Mt. xiii, 54]

2. [I believe in] God from God, light from light, true God from true God, begotten, not made.

3. We give thanks to God always for you all, recollecting (you) in our prayers, without interruption mindful of your work of faith and (your) labor of love. [I Thess. i, 2–3]

4. O the priceless love of charity: in order that you might redeem a slave, you handed over (your) Son.

5. And the glory of God shone around them. [Lk. ii, 9]

6. My time is not yet present, but your time has always been provided. [Jn. vii, 6]

7. He who loves (his) father and mother more than me is not worthy of me. [Mt. x, 37]

8. Pilate therefore said to them: "Take him, you, and according to your law judge him!" [Jn. xviii, 31]

9. For you were bought with a price! Therefore glorify God in your body. [I Cor. vi, 20]

10. Therefore he who loosens one of the least of these commandments and so teaches men, he shall be called least in the kingdom of heaven. [Mt. v, 19]

11. Pilate answered: "Am *I* a Jew?" [Jn. xviii, 35]

12. I have placed you for a light for the Gentiles. [Acts xiii, 47]

13. If you loved me, you would rejoice that I go to the Father, because the Father is greater than I. [Jn. xiv, 28]

14. For my yoke is sweet. [Mt. xi, 30]

15. It is more blessed to give than to receive. [Acts xx, 35]

16. "Simon (son) of John, do you love me more than these?" He [Simon] says to him: "Indeed, Lord, you know that I love you." He [Jesus] says to him: "Feed my lambs." [Jn. xxi, 15]

17. He comes therefore to Simon Peter. He [Peter] says to him: "Lord, do *you* wash my feet?" Jesus answers and says to him: "What I am doing you do not know just now, but afterwards you will know." Peter says to him: "You will not wash my feet ever!" Jesus answers him: "If I do not wash you, you do not have a part with me." Simon Peter says to him: "Lord, not only my feet, but also (my) hands and head!" [Jn. xiii, 6–9]

18. Isaiah said these things because he saw his glory and spoke about him. [Jn. xii, 41]

19. Lord, we know not where you are going; how can we know the way? [Jn. xiv, 5]

20. The wind blows where it wills, and you hear its voice, but you do not know from where it comes and where it goes; thus is every one who is born of the Spirit. [Jn. iii, 8]

21. And he [Jesus] said to him: "I will come and I will heal him." And in response, the centurion said: "Lord, I am not worthy that you enter under my roof, but only speak with a word, and my boy will be healed. For I also am a man under authority, having soldiers under me, and I say to this one: 'Go,' and he goes, and to another: 'Come,' and he comes, and to my servant: 'Do this,' and he does it." But hearing (him) Jesus was amazed and to (those) following him he said, "Amen I say to you: Never have I found such faith in Israel." [Mt. viii, 7–10]

22. Lord, let my prayer be directed like incense in your sight.

23. Pilate says to them: "What therefore am I to do about Jesus, who is called the Christ?" They all say: "Let him be crucified!" And he says: "But what evil has he done?" But they kept crying out more saying: "Let him be crucified!" [Mt. xxvii, 22–23]

24. But let every person be quick to hear, but slow to speak and slow to anger; for the anger of a man does not perform the justice of God. [James i, 19–20]

25. I will go around your altar, Lord, so that I may hear the sound of your praise.

26. I always taught in the synagogue and in the temple, where all the Jews meet. [Jn. xviii, 20]

27. Where is this (man) about to go, that we will not find him? [Jn. vii, 35]

28. [And you decreed him (to be) over the works of your hands.] [Heb. ii, 7]

29. Simon Peter says to him: "Lord, where are you going?" Jesus answers: "Where I go, you are not able now to follow me, but you will follow afterwards." [Jn. xiii, 36]

30. Purchase those things which we have need of for the festive day. [Jn. xiii, 29]

31. Amen I say to you: A greater one than John the Baptist has not arisen among the children of women; but he who is least in the kingdom of heaven is greater than that one. [Mt. xi, 11]

32. At that time answering Jesus said: "I confess to you, Father, the Lord of heaven and of earth." [Mt. xi, 25]

33. From where was the baptism of John? From heaven or from men? [Mt. xxi, 25]

34. But they were urging with great voices demanding that he be crucified. [Lk. xxiii, 23]

35. But the greatest of these is love. [I Cor. xiii, 13]

36. You are better than many sparrows. [Mt. x, 31]

37. They decided that Paul and Barnabas should go up (to Jerusalem). [Acts xv, 2]

38. Going (forth) therefore, teach all nations. [Mt. xxviii, 19]

39. Brethren, you know that from ancient days God chose among you for the Gentiles to hear through my mouth the word of the gospel and to believe. [Acts xv, 7]

40. He who is about to come after me was made before me, because he was before me. [Jn. i, 15]

41. O happy fault, which deserved to have such and so great a Redeemer!

42. You know how to discern the face of the sky, but you cannot (discern) the signs of the times. [Mt. xvi, 3]

43. And my spirit rejoiced in God my savior. [Lk. i, 47]

44. And received into the odor of sweetness, may he be mingled with the heavenly lights!

45. Praise the Lord, all nations; praise him, all peoples. [Ps. cxvii, 1]

II.   1. Quod mandātum est maximum omnium?

2. Majōrēs et sacerdōtēs templī Jēsūm observābant ut vidērent quid factūrus esset.

3. Suāvior odor hujus incēnsī, ā tē beātī, ad tē ascendat, O Domine.

4. Quid est majus quam dīlēctiō Deī et proximī?

Readings

1.   The Marriage Feast at Cana, Jn. ii, 1–11.

On the third day a marriage was performed in Cana of Galilee, and the mother of Jesus was there; and Jesus was invited to the wedding and his disciples (as well). And when the wine was running out, the mother of Jesus says to him: "They do not have wine." And Jesus says to her: "What (is it) to me and to you, woman? My hour has not yet come." His mother says to the servants: "Whatever he says to you, do." And there were six water-jars made of stone placed there according to the ceremonial washing of the Jews, each one holding two or three measures. Jesus says to them: "Fill up the jars with water." And they filled them up to the top. And he says to them: "Draw out now and bring (it) to the head waiter." And they brought (it). And when the head waiter tasted the water become wine and did not know from where it was—but the servants, who drew out the water, knew—the head waiter calls the bridegroom and says to him: "Every man serves first the good wine and, when (his guests) have been made drunk, (he serves) that which is less good; you have saved the good wine until now." This the first of (his) signs Jesus did in Cana of Galilee and revealed his glory, and his disciples believed in him.

2.   Queen of heaven, rejoice, alleluia,
      because the one whom you deserved to carry, alleluia,
      has arisen as he said, alleluia,
      pray to God for us, alleluia.

3.   The Family of Jesus, Mk. iii, 31–35.

      And his mother comes and his brothers, and standing outside they sent for him calling him. And a crowd was sitting around him, and they say to him: "Behold, your mother and your brothers and your sisters ask for you outside." And answering he said to them: "Who is my mother, and (who are) my brothers?" And looking around at those who were sitting in his circle, he said: "Behold my mother and my brothers. For whoever does the will of God, this one is my brother and my sister and mother."

Unit 28

Drills

I.
1. Pontius Pilate freed himself from blame.

2. The apostles will not carry the loaves with themselves.

3. The woman was giving to herself to drink.

4. Mindful of themselves they feared Jesus.

5. They were confessing their own sins.

6. On behalf of his own mother Jesus changed the water into wine.

7. Jesus was betrayed by one of his own apostles.

8. His/her daughter lost her own book.

9. Jesus knew in his very self the strength which had gone out from him.

10. Peter entered into the house, and his own (people) were there.

II.
1. Although she was a Samaritan, Jesus spoke to the woman.

2. When Peter was in Jerusalem, he saw Paul.

3. When they had dined, they went out of the house.

4. When/since they were called, they followed the Lord.

5. The women were suffering greatly, when/since they saw Jesus crucified.

Exercises

I. 1. When therefore he came into Galilee, the Galilaeans welcomed him, since they had seen all the things which he had done in Jerusalem on the feast day. [Jn. iv, 45]

2. And when he had said these things, with his knees bent / having knelt down, he prayed with them all. [Acts xx, 36]

3. But one of them, when he saw that he was healed, went back glorifying God with a loud voice. [Lk. xvii, 15]

4. How is a man able to be born, when he is old? [Jn. iii, 4]

5. But when he had come down from the mountain, many crowds followed him. [Mt. viii, 1]

6. Why does this (man) speak so? He blasphemes! Who is able to forgive sins except God alone? [Mk. ii, 7]

7. But one of his disciples said to him: Lord, allow me first to go and to bury my father." [Mt. viii, 21]

8. And Jesus responded to him: "It is written: '*Not on bread alone will man live*[, but on every word of God].'" [Lk. iv, 4]

9. And when he had arrived and had seen the grace of God, he rejoiced.

10. Great is the truth, and it prevails when many, infected by the devil, contradict it.

11. And going forth from there he saw two other brothers, James (the son) of Zebedee and his brother John, in a boat with their father Zebedee mending their nets, and he called them. [Mt. iv, 21]

12. For he who wishes to save his own life will lose it; but he who loses his own life for my sake, this one will save it. [Lk. ix, 24]

13. One yields to grave temptation, another does not.

14. And (though) finding no cause for death, they asked Pilate that he be killed. [Acts xiii, 28]

15. But seeing the crowds, he went up to the mountain; and when he had sat down, his disciples approached him. [Mt. v, 1]

16. The woman does not have power over her own body, but the man (does); and similarly the man also does not have power over his own body, but the woman (does). [I Cor. vii, 4]

17. He who is not with me is against me. [Mt. xii, 30]

18. The Lord will free me from every wicked deed and will make me safe into his heavenly kingdom; and to him glory forever. Amen. [II Tim. iv, 18]

19. Against you alone have I sinned, and I have done evil in your presence. [Ps. li, 4]

20. The sad women, suffering greatly, asked for quiet.

21. Amen, amen I say to you: The servant is not greater than his master, nor the apostle greater than he who sent him. [Jn. xiii, 16]

22. And Jesus returned in the power of the Spirit into Galilee. And a report went out through all the region concerning him. And he himself taught in their synagogues and he was glorified by all. [Lk. iv, 14–15]

23. And all in the synagogue were filled with anger hearing these things. [Lk. iv, 28]

24. Because of his protection of us, let us worship the Lord.

25. But rising from the synagogue, he went into the house of Simon. [Lk. iv, 38]

26. My country is much dearer to me than my life.

27. The priest concluded his own preface together with the people.

28. For he who eats and drinks, (while) not discerning the body, eats and drinks judgment upon himself. [I Cor. xi, 29]

29. But I want you all to speak in tongues, but even more to prophesy; for greater is he who prophesies than he who speaks in tongues. [I Cor. xiv, 5]

30. For he who speaks in a tongue, speaks not to men, but to God; for no one hears him, but he speaks mysteries in the spirit. [I Cor. xiv, 2]

31. This night puts to flight hatreds and humbles empires.

32. And if I hand over my body so that I may boast, but I have not love, it avails me nothing. [I Cor. xiii, 3]

33. Again he sent other servants, more than the previous (ones), and they did to them similarly. [Mt. xxi, 36]

34. Although you do not see [Jesus], you love (him). [I Pet. i, 8]

35. But Jesus answered nothing more, so that Pilate was amazed. [Mk. xv, 5]

36. And you, child, will be called the prophet of the Most High: for you will go *before the face of the Lord to prepare his ways, . . . to give light to those who sit in darkness and in the shadow of death,* to direct our feet onto the path of peace. [Lk. i, 76, 79]

37. And Mary said: "My soul extols the Lord." [Lk. i, 46]

38. You, Lord, in the beginning founded the earth; and the works of your hands are of heaven. [Heb. i, 10]

39. But he said to him: *"You shall love the Lord your God with your whole heart and with your whole soul* and with your whole mind: this is the greatest and the first commandment. And the second is similar to this: *You shall love your neighbor as yourself."* [Mt. xxii, 37–39]

40. May the Lord enkindle in us the fire of his love and the flame of eternal charity.

41. And they said to one another: "Was not our heart burning in us, while he spoke on the road and opened the Scriptures to us?" [Lk. xxiv, 32]

42. I sent you to reap that which you did not labor for; others have labored, and you have come into their labor. [Jn. iv, 38]

43. For it is better to suffer (while) doing good, if the will of God wills (it), than (to suffer while) doing evil. [I Pet. iii, 17]

44. And therefore having so great a cloud of witnesses placed around us, setting aside every burden and sin standing around us, let us with patience run the contest proposed to us. [Heb. xii, 1]

45. And when the Lord had seen her, moved with pity for her, he said to her: "Do not weep!" [Lk. vii, 13]

46. For what does it profit a man if he should gain the whole world and bring about the loss of his soul? [Mk. viii, 36]

47. For the Son of man is going to come in the glory of his Father together with his angels. [Mt. xvi, 27]

48. But John, when he had heard (while) in chains about the works of Christ, sending (word) by his disciples he said to him: "Are you he who is to come, or should we look for another?" [Mt. xi, 2–3]

49. And Jesus went about all Galilee, teaching in their synagogues and preaching the gospel of the kingdom. [Mt. iv, 23]

50. For Jesus himself provided witness that a prophet has no honor in his own country. [Jn. iv, 44]

51. If you wish to be perfect, go, sell what you have, and give (it) to the poor. [Mt. xix, 21]

52. The woman says to him: "I know that the Messiah is coming— the one who is called Christ—; when he comes, he will announce all things to us." [Jn. iv, 25]

53. Some were saying: "This is the Christ!" but certain ones were saying: "The Christ does not come from Galilee, does he?" [Jn. vii, 41]

54. At the words which follow, up to *factus est*, all should bow.

II. 1. Aliī linguīs loquuntur; aliī evangelizant. Dōna enim Spīrītūs Sānctī sunt multa.

2. Cum verba Jēsū audīvimus, dīligāmus invicem.

3. Nūlla spēs est prō illīs quī Patrem suum nōn invocant.

4. Diāconus dēvōtissimē ōrāvit ut Deus mēntēs nostrās et corda reficeret.

Readings

1. The Calling of the First Apostles, Mk. i, 16–20.

   And passing along the sea of Galilee he saw Simon and Andrew the brother of Simon casting [nets] into the sea; for they were fishermen. And Jesus said to them: "Come after me, and I will make you to become fishers of men." And right away, with the nets left behind, they followed him. And going on a little he saw James (the son) of Zebedee and John his brother, and (he saw) them in a boat mending nets, and immediately he called them. And, with their own father Zebedee left behind in the boat with hired men, they left him.

2. Two Blind Men, Mt. ix, 27–31.

   And with Jesus passing through from there, two blind (men) followed him, crying out and saying: "Have pity on us, son of David!" And when he had come to a house, the blind (men) came up to him, and Jesus says to them: "Do you believe that I am able to do this?" They say to him: "Certainly, Lord." Then he touched their eyes saying: "Accordng to your faith let it be done to you." And their eyes were opened. And Jesus sternly warned them saying: "See (to it) that no one knows." But going away they spread the news concerning him in all that land.

Unit 29

Drills

I. 1. Whatever you do to the least, you do to me.

2. Did Peter speak to someone on the road?

3. If you see anything, tell me.

4. Some woman left a book for you.

5. Whoever have ears, let them hear.

6. Were you asking for something good?

7. A certain (man) approached Jesus.

8. Gold was given to some soldiers.

II. 1. When (his) hour came, Jesus was praying.

2. Before you leave, go to Peter.

3. Because he was old, John was not able to go with (his) brothers.

4. Since he wished to hear Jesus, the man entered the synagogue.

5. Although he baptized not at all, Paul still preached the Gospel.

6. Even though they were sinners, Jesus ate with them.

7. When Jesus climbed the mountain to pray, the apostles followed him.

8. Because Jesus is our Savior, we praise him always and everywhere.

Exercises

I.   1. O good Jesus, have pity on us because you have created us, you have redeemed us with your most precious blood.

2. Jesus, Savior of the world, I have come to help your servants whom you have redeemed with your precious blood.

3. And you will be hated by all nations because of my name. [Mt. xxiv, 9]

4. They were kissing him grieving very greatly at the word which he had spoken, that they were not going to see his face any more. [Acts xx, 38]

5. Jacob I have loved, but Esau I have hated. [Rom. ix, 13]

6. For although I was free of all, I made myself the slave of all. [I Cor. ix, 19]

7. Although Jesus did not baptize, yet his disciples (did). [Jn. iv, 2]

8. For who knows the mind of the Lord so as to instruct him? But we have the mind of Christ. [I Cor. ii, 16]

9. Do we therefore destroy the law through faith? Far be it, but we uphold the law. [Rom. iii, 31]

10. For we have heard him saying that this Jesus of Nazareth will destroy this place and will change the customs which Moses handed down to us. [Acts vi, 14]

11. But if we judged ourselves, we would certainly not be judged, [I Cor. xi, 31]

12. You have crowned him with glory and honor[, and you have decreed him (to be) over the works of your hands]. [Heb. ii, 7]

13. And this is the testimony of John, when the Jews sent to him priests and Levites from Jerusalem in order to ask him: "Who are you?" [Jn. i, 19]

14. And Nathanael said to him: "Can anything good come out of Nazareth?" And Philip says to him: "Come and see." [Jn. i, 46]

15. Lord, come down before my boy dies. [Jn. iv, 49]

16. For the Father loves the Son and shows all things to him which he makes, and he will show to him works greater than these, so that you may be amazed. For just as the Father raises the dead and gives them life, so also the Son gives life to whom he wishes. [Jn. v, 20–21]

17. Amen, amen I say to you: The hour comes, and is now, when the dead will hear the voice of the Son of God, and those who hear will live. For just as the Father has life in himself, so he has given also to the Son to have life in himself; and he has given power to him also to pass judgment, because he is the Son of man. [Jn. v, 25–27]

18. I have come in the name of my Father, and you do not receive me; if another comes in his own name, you will receive him. [Jn. v, 43]

19. For this one was going to betray him, although he was one of the Twelve. [Jn. vi, 71]

20. But many of the crowd believed in him and were saying: "When the Christ comes, will he make more signs than those which this one has made?" [Jn. vii, 31]

21. But because I speak the truth you do not believe me. [Jn. viii, 45]

22. Therefore the Father loves me because I lay down my life so that I may obtain it again. [Jn. x, 17]

23. But when the fullness of time came, God sent his own Son, born of woman, made under the law, so that he might redeem those who were under the law. [Gal. iv, 4–5]

24. And while they were eating, he took bread and blessing (it) broke and gave (it) to them and said: "Take (it); this is my body." And with the cup received, giving thanks he gave (it) to them, and they all drank from it. And he said to them: "This is my blood of the new covenant, which is poured out for many." [Mk. xiv, 22–24]

25. But this is the will of the one who has sent me, so that everything which he has given to me I may not lose (any) of it, but I may raise it up on the last day. [Jn. vi, 39]

26. May my prayer, Lord, be directed like incense in your sight: the elevation of my hands, an evening sacrifice. [Ps. cxli, 2]

27. But God-fearing men buried Stephen and made a great mourning over him. [Acts viii, 2]

28. But even if we or an angel from heaven should preach to you (a gospel) contrary to (the gospel) which we have preached to you, let him be anathema! [Gal. i, 8]

29. I confess to God almighty and to you, brothers, that I have sinned much in thought, in word, in deed, and by omission.

30. The psalmist or a cantor says the psalm.

31. At the conclusion of Mass the people cry out: Thanks (be) to God.

32. Jesus has wiped away the debt of old sin with his holy blood.

33. Therefore in the grace of this night, take, holy Father, the evening sacrifice of this incense.

34. Therefore may the sanctification of this night put to flight sins, wash faults: and give back innocence to the fallen and joy to the sad.

35. Let the deacon kindle this precious lamp!

36. The humble guests are filled with fear.

37. And Jesus increased in wisdom and in age and in favor with God and men. [Lk. ii, 52]

38. May all the earth worship you (as) the eternal Father.

39. After this Mary Magdalene recognized Jesus.

40. And when you stand in prayer, forgive, if you have anything against anyone, so that your Father also, who is in heaven, may forgive you your sins. [Mk. xi, 25]

41. And he said to his disciples: "Sit here while I pray." And he takes Peter and James and John with him. [Mk. xiv, 32–33]

42. Give back to all (their) dues: . . . respect to whom (you owe) respect, honor to whom (you owe) honor. [Rom. xiii, 7]

43. O how many, of what kind (are) those Sabbaths, Which the heavenly court always celebrates. [Peter Abelard]

44. Behold the figure of Jesus, increasing until he embraces the whole world.

45. Let us humbly beseech God and let us conduct ourselves well.

46. But this is the judgment: Light came into the world, and men loved darkness more than light; for their works were evil. [Jn. iii, 19]

II. 1. Quamquam discipulī pānem multum emere nōn possent, tōta turba aliquid habuit mandūcāre.

    2. Cum Jēsūs ā Patre missus esset, mōnstrāvit apostolīs evangelizāre.

    3. Quandō Jēsūs calicem cēpit, eum benedīxit et apostolīs dedit.

    4. Postquam in caelum assūmpta est, Marīa glōriā et honōre corōnāta est.

    5. Priusquam sanguine pretiōsō redēmptī sumus, nūllam spem salūtārem habuimus.

Readings

1. The Second Sign at Cana, Jn. iv, 46–54.

    He came therefore again into Cana of Galilee, where he (had) made the water wine. And there was a certain royal official whose son was sick at Capernaum; when this (man) had heard that Jesus had arrived from Judea into Galilee, he went away to him and asked that he come down and heal his son; for he was beginning to die. Jesus therefore said to him: "Unless you see signs and wonders, you will not believe." The royal official says to him: "Lord, come down before my son dies."

Jesus says to him: "Go, your son lives." The man believed in the word which Jesus said to him and he went. But when he was going down, his servants ran up to him saying that his boy lived. He therefore asked them the hour in which (his son) got better. So they said to him: "Yesterday at the seventh hour the fever left him." So the father knew that it was at that hour that Jesus said to him: "Your son lives," and he believed and his whole house (believed). This again (was) a second sign (that) Jesus did , when he had come from Judea into Galilee.

2.   The Conditions for Following Jesus, Mt. viii, 19–22.

And approaching, one scribe said to him: "Teacher, I will follow you wherever you go." And Jesus says to him: "Foxes have lairs and birds of the sky (have) nests, but the Son of man does not have (a place) where he may recline (his) head." But another of his disciples said to him: "Lord, allow me first to go and to bury my father." But Jesus said to him: "Follow me and permit the dead to bury their own dead."

Unit 30

Drills

I. 1. Do not conduct yourselves in that manner!

2. May they not take the cup unworthily!

3. You shall not kill!

4. Do not speak!

5. Go, do not sin any more!

6. Do not awaken your father!

7. Do not pour my wine into your cups!

8. Let us not be sad!

II. 1a. I know that my Redeemer lives.
1b. Redēmptor meus vīvit. / My Redeemer lives.

2a. Jesus revealed to them that he was going to die.
2b. Ego moritūrus sum. / I am going to die.

3a. They said that they (themselves) were able to destroy the temple.
3b. Templum dēstruere possumus. / We are able to destroy the temple.

4a. They said that they (those others) were able to destroy the temple.
4b. Templum dēstruere possunt. / They are able to destroy the temple.

5a. He/she said that they knew Peter.
5b. Petrum cognōscunt. / They know Peter.

6a. The host believed that he had more wine.
6b. Plūs vīnī habeō. / I have more wine.

7a. We knew that he was being praised by Paul.
7b. Laudātur ā Paulō. / He is being praised by Paul.

8a. The women saw that Jesus was being crucified.
8b. Jēsūs crucifīgitur. / Jesus is being crucified.

9a. Do you say that faith grows with praying?
9b. Fidēs ōrandō crēscit. / Faith grows with praying.

10a. They had heard that Jesus was in the city.
10b. Jēsūs est in cīvitāte. / Jesus is in the city.

11a. Do you wish to tell me that Peter is the greatest of the apostles?
11b. Maximus apostolōrum est Petrus. / Peter is the greatest of the
    apostles.

Exercises

I.   1. Fear nothing of these things which you are about to suffer. [Rev.
        ii, 10]

     2. These things the Holy (one), the True (one) speaks, who has *the
        key of David, who opens and no one will close, and closes and no
        one opens.* [Rev. iii, 7]

     3. But he denied in the presence of all, saying: "I know not what
        you say." [Mt. xxvi, 70]

     4. Do not wonder at this, that the hour comes in which all who are
        in (their) graves will hear his voice and go forth, those who have
        done good into the resurrection of life, and those who have
        surely done evil into the resurrection of judgment. [Jn. v, 28–29]

     5. But they, when they saw him walking on the sea, thought he was
        a ghost and cried out. [Mk. vi, 49]

     6. Count everything a joy, my brothers, when you happen upon
        various temptations. [James i, 2]

7. And at once, while he is still speaking, Judas one of the Twelve comes, and with him a crowd with swords and clubs. [Mk. xiv, 43]

8. And he said to them: "Sad is my spirit unto death." [Mk. xiv, 34]

9. But while he was thinking these things, behold, an angel of the Lord appeared in his dreams, saying to him: "Joseph son of David, do not be afraid to receive Mary as your wife. For that which is born in her is from the Holy Spirit; moreover, she will give birth to a son, and you will call his name Jesus: for he will save his people from their sins." [Mt. i, 20–21]

10. Owe nothing to anyone, except that you love one another: for he who loves his neighbor has fulfilled the law. [Rom. xiii, 8]

11. For it availed us nothing to be born, unless it had availed us to be redeemed . . . O priceless love of charity!

12. This is the night which, today through all the world, gives back to grace, connects to sanctity those believing in Christ, (who are) separated from the vices of the world and from the gloom of sins.

13. For he is nourished by the melting waxes.

14. You examine the Scriptures because you think you have eternal life in them; and they are what produce testimony about me. And you are not willing to come to me so that you may have eternal life. [Jn. v, 39–40]

15. Do not think that I am going to accuse you in the presence of the Father; there is one who accuses you: Moses, in whom you hope. [Jn. v, 45]

16. Although fire may be divided into parts, it does not know losses of light.

17. But brother will betray brother unto death, and father son; and sons will rise against their parents and will affect them with death. And you will be hated by all because of my name; but he who perseveres to the end, this one will be saved. [Mt. x, 21–22]

18. Therefore we pray you, Lord: that this Candle, consecrated for the honor of your name, may continue unfailing(ly) to destroy the gloom of this night.

19. You have heard that it is said: "*You shall love your neighbor* and you shall hold your enemy in hatred." But I say to you: Love your enemies and pray for those who persecute you. [Mt. v, 43–44]

20. Daughters of Jerusalem, do not weep over me, but weep over yourselves and over your sons. [Lk. xxiii, 28]

21. No one has a greater love than this, that he put down his life for his friends. You are my friends, if you do (the things) which I command you. [Jn. xv, 13–14]

22. And no one was able to answer a word to him, nor did anyone dare from that day to question him more. [Mt. xxii, 46]

23. Do and observe all things, therefore, whatever they say to you; but do not act according to their works: for they say but do not do / preach but do not practice. [Mt. xxiii, 3]

24. Jesus says to her: Do not touch me, for I have not yet ascended to my Father: but go to my brothers, and say to them: I ascend to my Father and your Father, and my God and your God. [Jn. xx, 17]

25. And they answered that they did not know from where it was. [Lk. xx, 7]

26. I will rise and I will go to my father and I will say to him: Father, I have sinned against heaven and in your presence and now I am not worthy to be called your son. [Lk. xv, 18–19]

27. And when they had seen that certain of his disciples, with un clean hands, that is, not washed, were eating bread[, they scolded (them)]. [Mk. vii, 2]

28. Whether therefore you eat or you drink or you do anything else, do all for the glory of God. [I Cor. x, 31]

29. But Paul cried out with a great voice saying: Do nothing evil to yourself, for we are all here. [Acts xvi, 28]

30. Brothers, do not become children in (your) thoughts. [I Cor. xiv, 20]

31. But praying / as you pray, do not speak too much. [Mt. vi, 7]

32. Do not think that I have come to destroy the Law or the Prophets; I have not come to destroy but to fulfill. [Mt. v, 17]

33. And with it immediately understood in his spirit that they were so thinking among themselves, Jesus says to them: "Why do you think these things in your hearts?" [Mk. ii, 8]

34. Do not judge according to appearance, but judge a just judgment. [Jn. vii, 24]

35. And knowing this time, that the hour is now for us [sic] to arise from sleep, for salvation is now nearer to us than when we (first) believed. [Rom. xiii, 11]

36. The Son of man must be betrayed into the hands of men. [Mt. xvii, 22]

37. And on the way he was questioning his disciples, saying to them: "Who do men say that I am?" [Mk. viii, 27]

38. And he himself was questioning them: "Truly who do you say that I am?" Answering, Peter said to him: "You are the Christ." [Mk. viii, 29]

39. Heaven and earth will pass away, but my words will not pass away. But concerning the day or the hour, no one knows, neither the angels in heaven nor the Son except the Father. [Mk. xiii, 31–32]

40. And crying out with a loud voice Jesus said: "Father, *into your hands I commend my spirit*"; and saying this he died. [Lk. xxiii, 46]

41. But he said: "Amen I say to you: No prophet is received in his own country." [Lk. iv, 24]

42. But since Jesus knew their thoughts, answering he said to them: "What are you thinking in your hearts? Which is easier to say, 'Your sins are forgiven you,' or to say, 'Arise and walk'?" [Lk. v, 22–23]

43. And do not judge and you will not be judged. [Lk. vi, 37]

44. O sacred heart of Jesus, draw me after you!

45. Our Lady is called the seat of wisdom. For ineffable is Mary's understanding of divinity.

46. When the day became light, Jesus went around to nearby places.

47. Were not Roman soldiers forbidden to oppress the Jews?

48. Grace, mercy, and peace will be with us from God the Father and from Jesus Christ, Son of the Father, in truth and love. [II Jn. 3]

49. But the demons went out from many, crying out and saying: "You are the Son of God." And rebuking (them) he was not allowing them to speak, because they knew that he was the Christ. [Lk. iv, 41]

50. For I decided that I did not know anything among you except Jesus Christ and him crucified. [I Cor. ii, 2]

51. But the spiritual (man) judges all, and he himself is judged by no one. [I Cor. ii, 15]

II.   1. Rogātus Petrus negāvit sē scīre Jēsūm.

2. Nōlī cōnārī lignum dētrahere sōlus!

3. Difficile est exprimere dolōrem nostrum ad mortem amīcī.

4. Nōlīte putāre quia vōs nōn debeātis inimīcōs vestrōs dīligere.

5. Sī persevērāveris Dominum serviēns, gaudium et pāx tibi erunt.

6. Exīstimāvērunt amīcī nostrī quia difficile esset vetāre inimīcōs in cīvitātem intrāre?

Readings

1. Lavabo, Ps. xxvi, 6–12.

    I will wash my hands among the innocent and I will go around your altar, Lord,

    So that I may hear the voice of praise and tell all your wonderful things.

    Lord, I have loved the beauty of your house and the place of dwelling of your glory.

Do not destroy my soul with the wicked, God, and my life with men
   of blood,
In whose hands are iniquities: their right hands are filled with bribes.
But I have walked along in my innocence; redeem me and have pity
   on me.
My foot has stood on the straight line; in the assemblies I will bless
   you, Lord.

2.   Expulsion of the Devils in Gerasa (I), Mk. v, 1–10.

And they came across the strait of the sea into the country of the Ger-
asenes. And when he came out from the boat, there met him immediately from the tombs a man of unclean spirit, who had his dwelling
in the tombs; nor was anyone now able to restrain him with chains,
because, though often bound with leg irons and chains, he had shat-
tered the chains and broken the leg irons into small pieces, and no
one was able to subdue him; and always by night and by day he was
in the tombs and in the mountains, crying out and gashing himself
with stones. And seeing Jesus at a distance, he ran up and worshipped
him and crying out with a loud voice said: "What (is there) to me and
to you / What have you to do with me, Jesus, Son of the Most High
God? I implore you through God, do not torture me." For he [Jesus]
was saying to him: "Come out from the man, unclean spirit." And
he asked him: "What is your name?" And he said to him: "Legion is
my name, because we are many." And he beseeched him much not to
drive him out of the country.

Unit 31

Drills

I. 1a. The deacon believed that he had been appointed.
    1b. Ego dēputātus sum. / I have been appointed.

2a. Do you believe that God parted the sea for the Hebrews?
2b. Deus prō Hebraeīs mare dīvīsit. / God parted the sea for the Hebrews.

3a. We know that Lucifer has shone upon all.
3b. Lūcifer omnibus illūxit. / Lucifer has shone upon all.

4a. It was said that the crowd had forbidden Pilate to release Jesus.
4b. Turba vetuit Pīlātum Jēsūm dīmittere. / The crowd forbade Pilate to release Jesus.

5a. These (men) say that John was not Christ.
5b. Jōannēs nōn erat Chrīstus. / John was not Christ.

6a. Mary Magdalene did not see that Jesus had arisen from the dead.
6b. Jēsūs ā mortuīs resurrēxit. / Jesus arose from the dead.

7a. The man was forbidden to say that he had been healed by Jesus.
7b. Ego ā Jēsū sānātus sum. / I have been healed by Jesus.

8a. Let no one say to anyone that Paul baptized.
8b. Paulus baptizāvit. / Paul baptized.

9a. Don't they know that Mary expressed such sorrow with abundant tears?

9b. Marīa amplīs expressit lacrimīs tālem dolōrem. / Mary expressed such sorrow with abundant tears.

10a. He/she thought he had seen Jesus on the road.
He/she thought Jesus had seen him on the road.

10b. Ego Jēsūm in viā vīdi. / I saw Jesus on the road.
Eum Jēsūs in viā vīdit. / Jesus saw him on the road.

II.   1. He who says this is too humble.

2. Whatever they did, they did on behalf of (their) friends.

3. They who should do this would be pleasing to the Father.

4. Where you wish to go, I will follow.

5. Whoever had asked would have received.

Exercises

I.   1. And he said: "What evil has he done?" But they cried out more, saying: "Let him be crucified!" [Mt. xxvii, 23]

2. He who believes in the Son has life eternal, but he who is unbelieving in the Son will not see life, but the wrath of God remains over him. [Jn. iii, 36]

3. "Do you think you understand what you are reading?" And he said: "How can I, if no one shows me?" [Acts viii, 30–31]

4. And the whole crowd sought to touch him, because a strength was coming out of him and was healing all. [Lk. vi, 19]

5. But after John was betrayed, Jesus came into Galilee preaching the gospel of God, and saying: "The time is fulfilled, and the kingdom of God has approached; repent and believe in the gospel." [Mk. i, 14–15]

6. Having returned from hell, he shone bright(ly) on the human race.

7. Through the same Lord of ours Jesus Christ, your Son: who lives and reigns with you in the unity of the Holy Spirit, God: for ever and ever. Amen.

8. Just as she conceived (being) a holy virgin, (so) Mary gave birth (as) a virgin, (and) a virgin she remained.

9. How can you believe, if you seek glory from one another and do not seek the glory which is from God alone? [Jn. v, 44]

10. Jesus therefore said to those Jews who believed in him: "If you stay in my word, you are truly my disciples and you will know the truth, and the truth will free you." [Jn. viii, 31–32]

11. Then they returned to Jerusalem from the mountain which is called Olivet. [Acts i, 12]

12. Repent therefore and turn around, so that your sins may be wiped out. [Acts iii, 19]

13. And so Jesus, knowing all the things which were about to come upon him, went forth and said to them: "Whom do you seek?" [Jn. xviii, 4]

14. [Do you not know of what sort of spirit you are?] [Lk. ix, 55]

15. Here now it is sought among the stewards whether any may be found (to be) trustworthy. [I Cor. iv, 2]

16. For the Father also seeks such who would worship him. [Jn. iv, 23]

17. They came saying that they themselves had seen even a vision of angels who say that he lives. [Lk. xxiv, 23]

18. Let not any evil talk come out of your mouth. [Eph. iv, 29]

19. Then Jesus said to him: "Turn around your sword into its place. For all who take the sword will perish by the sword." [Mt. xxvi, 52]

20. But I do not seek my glory; he is (the one) who seeks and judges. [Jn. viii, 50]

21. But Jesus stood before the procurator; and the procurator

questioned him saying: "Are you the king of the Jews?" Jesus says to him: "You say (so)." [Mt. xxvii, 11]

22. But the servant does not stay in the house forever; the son stays forever. [Jn. viii, 35]

23. Again therefore Jesus spoke to them saying: I am the light of the world; he who follows me will not walk in darkness, but he will have the light of life." [Jn. viii, 12]

24. Amen, amen I say to you: The hour is coming, and it is now, when the dead will hear the voice of the Son of God, and those who hear will live. [Jn. v, 25]

25. And standing Jesus [commands that he be called]. [Mk. x, 49]

26. If anyone has ears for hearing, let him hear. [Mk. iv, 23]

27. And he said: "He who has ears for hearing, let him hear." [Mk. iv, 9]

28. At the same time Moses was born, and he was handsome in the presence of God. [Acts vii, 20]

29. Then they suborned men to say [that they themselves had heard him speaking words of blasphemy] against Moses and God. [Acts vi, 11]

30. But when Jesus had been born in Bethlehem of Judea in the days of Herod the king, behold, magi from the east came to Jerusalem saying, "Where is he who was born king of the Jews? For we have seen his star in the east and we have come to worship him." [Mt. ii, 1–2]

31. Let women be silent in the churches, for it is not permitted for them to speak; but let them be submissive, just as the law says. [I Cor. xiv, 34]

32. The pope has his seat in the city of Rome.

33. And he said to her: "Because of this talk, go; the demon has left your daughter. [Mk. vii, 29]

34. They had not believed these who had seen him raised up. [Mk. xvi, 14]

35. Command therefore that the tomb be guarded up to the third day. [Mt. xxvii, 64]

36. And they say to her: "Woman, why are you weeping?" [Jn. xx, 13]

37. On the eighth day Jesus appeared to the apostles.

38. And while they were gazing into heaven as he went, behold, two men stood next to them in white clothes, who said: "Men of Galilee, why do you stand looking into heaven? This Jesus, who was taken from you into heaven, will so come just as you saw him going into heaven." [Acts i, 10–11]

39. And when the day of Pentecost was fulfilled, they were all together in the same place. [Acts ii, 1]

40. God raised his Son, with the sorrows of hell broken up.

41. O truly blessed night, which alone deserved to know the time and the hour in which Christ rose from hell!

42. Your redemption draws near. [Lk. xxi, 28]

43. The teacher was telling the pure and innocent children about the majesty of God.

44. But turning and seeing her Jesus said: "Take heart, daughter; your faith has saved you." [Mt. ix, 22]

45. Does not the disciple know that Christ the victor over death has arisen?

46. It is characteristic of the contrite man to express sorrow for (his) sins.

47. The man related to the people how much Jesus had done.

48. The elder to the elect lady and her children, whom I love in truth, and not I alone, but also all who know the truth, because of the truth, which abides in us and will be with us forever. [II Jn. 1–2. Note: This passage is an epistolary salutation, not a sentence. The "elder" is probably St. John, head of the early Christian communities in the province of Asia; the "lady" is probably a particular community in Asia.]

49. For who of men knows the things which are of man, except the spirit of man which is in him? So too the things which are of God no one knows except the Spirit of God. [I Cor. ii, 11]

II.　1.　Quīcumque, pār Magīs, stēllam sequātur, invenīre Rēgem Jūdaeōrum possit.

2.　Cum Paulus urbī appropinquābat, vōcem ē caelō subitō audīvit.

3.　Quīcumque fidēlis permānserit, nōn moriētur in aeternum.

4.　Regressus ad urbem Jēsūs ā turbā quaesītus est.

5.　Paulus dīcit fuisse bonae mulieris in ecclēsiīs tacēre.

Readings

1.　Easter Sequence [Wipo, 1048].

Let Christians offer praises
To the Paschal victim.
The Lamb has redeemed the sheep:
The blameless Christ to the Father
Has restored
Sinners.
Death and life in a wondrous battle
Have contended:
The leader of life, having died,
Reigns alive.
Tell us, Mary,
What have you seen on the road?
The tomb of the living Christ,
And the glory of (him) arising, I have seen:
The angels (as) witnesses,
The shroud and the clothing.
Christ has arisen
My hope:
He will go before you
Into Galilee.
We know that Christ has arisen
From the dead, truly:

You, victor King, on us
Have pity.
Amen. Alleluia.

2.   Expulsion of the Devils in Gerasa (II), Mk. v, 11–20.

And there around the mountain was a great herd of pigs feeding; and they begged him, saying: "Send us into the pigs, so that we may enter into them." And he yielded to them. And going out the unclean spirits entered into the pigs. And in a great rush, the herd, about two thousand (of them), fell over a precipice into the sea, and they were drowned in the sea. But the ones who were feeding them fled into the city and the fields and announced (what they had seen); and they came out to see what had happened. And they come to Jesus; and they see the one who was vexed by the demon, sitting, clothed, and of sound mind, him who had had legion, and they were afraid. And the ones who had seen told them how it had happened to him who had had the demon, and about the pigs. And they began to ask him [Jesus] to depart from their territory. And when he was going up into the boat, the one who had been vexed by the demon begged him to be with him. But he [Jesus] did not allow him, but said to him: "Go into your home to yours, and announce to them how much the Lord has done for you and has had mercy on you." And he went away and began to proclaim in Decapolis how much Jesus had done for him, and all were amazed.

Unit 32

Drills

I.   1a. Did the apostles know that Jesus was going to die?
      1b. Jēsūs moritūrus est. / Jesus is going to die.

    2a. The Magi did not see that the king would kill the children.
    2b. Rēx puerōs interfectūrus est. / The king is going to kill the
        children.

    3a. They understand that they will perish in the sea.
    3b. Peritūrī sumus in marī. / We are going to perish in the sea.

    4a. We perceived that Paul would stay in Rome.
    4b. Paulus mānsūrus est Rōmae. / Paul is going to stay in Rome.

    5a. He thought that she would be silent.
    5b. Ea tacitūra est. / She is going to be silent.

    6a. No one perceived that the Holy Spirit would descend over Jesus.
    6b. Spīritus Sānctus dēscēnsūrus est super Jēsūm. / The Holy Spirit is
        going to descend over Jesus.

II.   1. Jesus saw the crowds following him.

     2. Did Peter hear the man who was calling him?

     3. Paul blessed the man who cursed him.

     4. Jesus asked that the little ones be permitted to come to him.

Exercises

I.   1. But hearing (him) Jesus was amazed and he said to those following him: "Amen I say to you: In the presence of no one have I found such faith in Israel." [Mt. viii, 10]

2. God, raising up his own Child, sent him to you first, to bless you in turning each of you away from your evil ways. [Acts iii, 26]

3. And he was speaking the word openly. [Mk. viii, 32]

4. While he was praying, the appearance of (his) face was changed.

5. Eternal rest grant to them, Lord!

6. Jesus himself, approaching, went with them, but their eyes were restrained lest they recognize him. [Lk. xxiv, 15–16]

7. And when his own had heard, they went out to seize him. [Mk. iii, 21]

8. For John the Baptist came neither eating bread nor drinking wine, and you say: "He has a demon!" [Lk. vii, 33]

9. But he looked intently at them, hoping that he would receive something from them. [Acts iii, 5]

10. And (though) wishing to kill him, he feared the people because they considered him a prophet. [Mt. xiv, 5]

11. Gentle am I and humble of heart, and you will find rest for your souls. [Mt. xi, 29]

12. You have heard that it was said to the ancients: *You shall not kill.* [Mt. v, 21]

13. But hope which is seen is not hope; for who hopes for what he sees? [Rom. viii, 24]

14. What I say to you in shadows speak in the light; and what you hear in (your) ear preach on the rooftops. And fear not those who kill the body, but are not able to kill the soul. [Mt. x, 26–28]

15. But I praise you because in all respects you are mindful of me, and you cling to my traditions just as I have handed them down to you. [I Cor. xi, 2]

16. Each day I sat teaching in the temple, and you did not arrest me. [Mt. xxvi, 55]

17. But when we had entered Rome, it was permitted to Paul to stay by himself with a soldier guarding him. [Acts xxviii, 16]

18. And he took him up and showed to him all the kingdoms of the world. [Lk. iv, 5]

19. But some gave him palms on (his) face / slapped him. [Mt. xxvi, 67]

20. And he had received a response from the Holy Spirit that he would not see death unless first he saw the Lord's Christ. [Lk. ii, 26]

21. But he killed James the brother of John with a sword. [Acts xii, 2]

22. And with a response received in (their) dreams that they not re turn to Herod, they went back to their own country through an other route. And when they had gone back, behold, an angel of the Lord appears in the dreams of Joseph saying: "Arise and take the boy and his mother and flee into Egypt and be there until I speak to you; for it is about to happen that Herod will seek the boy in order to destroy him." [Mt. ii, 12–13]

23. For he is nourished by the melting waxes which the mother bee brought out into the substance of this precious lamp.

24. As the bees turn flowers into wax, so we ought to perform every thing for good.

25. For these are the paschal feasts, in which that true Lamb was killed, by whose blood the doorposts of the faithful are consecrated. This therefore is the night which has purged the darkness of sinners with the light of the pillar.

26. We hope it will come to be that we are at once forever nourished by your glory, through Christ our Lord, through whom you bestow all good things on the world.

27. May you deign to unite your church according to your will.

28. He has canceled the bill of an old sin with his holy blood.

29. On the last day all will be led before the throne to be judged.

30. In that book is contained the whole from which the world is to be judged.

31. O fountain of goodness, save me!

32. Make a gift of forgiveness before the day of reckoning.

33. By what clemency were you conquered?

34. We beseech you, therefore, assist your servants!

35. In you, Lord, have I hoped: may I not be confused forever!

36. Jesus, the judge of all, was beaten by the Roman soldiers.

37. The saint wrote about Jesus hanging on the saving cross.

38. May the Lord accept a sacrifice from your hands to the praise and glory of his name, for our benefit also and (for that) of his entire holy Church.

39. Whoever speaks against me speaks also against the Father, who is in heaven.

40. The priest begins to perform the Eucharistic liturgy.

41. Many, such as John, thought that the Antichrist would come out in the last days.

42. The Lord (is) my light and my salvation—whom shall I fear? [Ps. xxvii, 1]

II.   1. Chrīstus mortuus est ut mortem vinceret.

2. Crēdimus nōs ante thronum Deī statūrōs esse.

3. Aliquī virī missī sunt ad Jēsūm tenendum.

4. Jēsūs spērāvit apostolōs sē sustentūrōs esse.

5. Jēsūs praenōvit aliquōs virōs sē tentūrōs et verberātūrōs esse.

Readings

1. Tantum Ergo, by St. Thomas Aquinas (1225–1274).

    So great a sacrament, therefore,
    let us worship, bowing;
    and let the ancient example
    yield to the new rite;
    let faith accomplish a reinforcement
    for the failure of the senses.

    To the Father, and to the begotten
    (let there be) praise and a festal cry,
    salvation, honor, strength also
    let there be, and a blessing (as well):
    (and) to the one proceeding from both
    let there be equal praise.

2. Peter's Discourse in Caesarea (I), Acts x, 34–39.

    But opening (his) mouth Peter said: "In truth I discover that God is not a respector of persons, but in every nation the one who fears him and works justice is acceptable to him. He sent the word to the sons of Israel, preaching the gospel of peace through Jesus Christ; this one is the Lord of all. You know that the word was made/preached through all Judea, beginning from Galilee after the baptism which John preached: how God anointed Jesus of Nazareth with the Holy Spirit and with strength; and he went about doing good and healing all (who were) oppressed by the Devil, because God was with him. And we are witnesses of all things which he did in the country of the Jews and Jerusalem; and they killed him, hanging (him) up on a tree."

3. Mary Magdalen sees the risen Lord, Jn. xx, 15–18.

    Jesus said to her: "Woman, why are you weeping? Whom do you seek?" She, thinking that he was a gardener, said to him: "Master, if you have taken him away, tell me where you have put him, and I will take him." Jesus said to her: "Mary!" Turning she said to him in Hebrew: "Rabbuni!"—which is to say Teacher. Jesus said to her: "Do not hold me now, for I have not yet ascended to the Father; but go to my brothers and say to them: I am ascending to my Father and your Father, and my God and your God." Mary Magdalen came, announcing to the disciples: "I have seen the Lord!" and that he had said these things to her.

Unit 33

Drills

I.   1a. auferētur: "he/she/it will be taken away"
      1b. auferentur: "they will be taken away"

      2a. cōnfers: "you [sg.] (are) accompany(ing)"
      2b. cōnfertis: "you [pl.] (are) accompany(ing)"

      3a. dēferris: "you [sg.] are (being) brought"
      3b. dēferiminī: "you [pl.] are (being) brought"

      4a. efferēns: "bringing out"
      4b. efferentēs: "bringing out"

      5a. īnferunt: "they (are) bring(ing) in"
      5b. īnfert: "he/she/it brings in / is bringing in"

      6a. perferiminī: "you [pl.] are (being) carried through"
      6b. perferris: "you [sg.] are (being) carried through"

      7a. prōferimus: "we (are) bring(ing) forth"
      7b. prōferō: "I (am) bring(ing) forth"

      8a. refert: "he/she/it brings back / is bringing back"
      8b. referunt: "they (are) bring(ing) back"

      9a. offeram: "I will offer"
      9b. offerēmus: "we will offer"

9a. offeram: "I may offer"
9b. offerāmus: "we may offer" / "let us offer"

10a. referre: "you [sg.] are (being) brought back"
10b. referiminī: "you [pl.] are (being) brought back"

II.   1. on that day

       2. through (the) days

       3. on/at/during the eighth hour

       4. for eight days

       5. in/during seven years

       6. in/at that time

       7. in/at the last hour

Exercises

I.   1. Hail, Mary, full of grace, the Lord (is) with you; blessed (are) you
           among women, and blessed (is) the fruit of your womb [Lk. i, 28,
           42], Jesus. Holy Mary, Mother of God, pray for us sinners, now
           and at the hour of our death. Amen.

       2. If I should speak in the tongues of men and of angels, but do not
           have love, I have become like a gong sounding. [I Cor. xiii, 1]

       3. To signify the end of the reading, the reader adds: the Word of
           the Lord. R. Thanks (be) to God.

       4. On the Holy Sabbath, the deacon sang the Paschal Proclamation
           for the people.

       5. Pilate handed over Jesus that they might crucify (him) beaten
           with scourges.

       6. Let Christ the king of Israel descend now from the cross, so that
           we may see and believe. [Mk. xv, 32]

       7. Sing, tongue, the mystery of the glorious body, and of the
           precious blood, which the fruit of a noble womb, the king of
           nations, poured out for the ransom of the world. [St. Thomas
           Aquinas]

8. For he who has, to him will be given (more); and he who does not have, even what he has will be taken from him. [Mk. iv, 25]

9. May this Host avail to our reconciliation, we beseech (you), Lord, for the peace and salvation of the whole world.

10. The grace of our Lord Jesus Christ and the love of God and the fellowship of the Holy Spirit (be) with all of you. [II Cor. xiii, 13]

11. But in these days prophets came over from Jerusalem to Antioch; and rising one of them, by name Agabus, signified through the Spirit that there would be a great famine on all the earth. [Acts xi, 27–28]

12. They brought to him all who were sick and who had demons. [Mk. i, 32]

13. Merciful Father, in pity unite to yourself all your sons (who are) dispersed everywhere from you.

14. Jesus came and stood in their midst and said to them: "Peace (be) with you!" [Jn. xx, 19]

15. Although it may be divided into parts, nevertheless it knows not the loss of borrowed light.

16. He who is not with me is against me, and he who does not gather with me scatters. [Lk. xi, 23]

17. And they brought to him all who were sick. [Mt. iv, 24]

18. Why do you stand here idle all day? [Mt. xx, 6]

19. But in those days John the Baptist came, preaching in the desert of Judea. [Mt. iii, 1]

20. With the brothers having been found, we were asked to stay with them for seven days. [Acts xxviii, 14]

21. And they come bringing to him a paralytic, who was being carried by four (men). [Mk. ii, 3]

22. Amen I say to you: Wherever this gospel is preached in the whole world, what this (woman) has done will be said in memory of her. [Mt. xxvi, 13]

23. And he did not allow anyone to follow him except Peter and James and John the brother of James. [Mk. v, 37]

24. But when he was in Jerusalem on the Passover, on the feast day, many believed in his name, seeing his signs which he did. [Jn. ii, 23]

25. I am with you for so great a time and you have not come to know me, Philip? He who has seen me has seen the Father. Why do you say: "Show us the Father"? [Jn. xiv, 9]

26. But with Herod (being) dead, behold, an angel of the Lord appears in the dreams of Joseph in Egypt. [Mt. ii, 19]

27. For you bring certain wonderful things to our ears. [Acts xvii, 20]

28. Whoever does not receive the kingdom of God like a child, he will not enter into it. [Mk. x, 15]

29. Therefore those who had been scattered went about preaching the word. [Acts viii, 4]

30. But on the following day Paul went in with us to James, and all the elders were gathered. [Acts xxi, 18]

31. And immediately the Spirit drove him out into the desert. [Mk. i, 12]

32. O truly blessed night, which enriched the Hebrews!

33. O God, grant us a tranquil time of everlasting peace!

34. The mother was grieving while she saw the pains of (her) son wounded with beatings.

35. Let our praise be full and pleasing!

36. Good shepherd, make us companions of the saints!

37. You will not say a false testimony. [Mt. xix, 18]

38. Christ, the Second Adam, hung on a tree, so that he might abolish the punishments of the tree.

39. I will announce your name to my brothers, in the midst of the assembly I will praise you. [Heb. ii, 12]

40. The fire, I say, will be everlasting.

41. Immediately she fell down before his feet and died; but coming in, the young men found her dead: and they took (her) out and buried (her) beside her husband. [Acts v, 10]

42. But Mary kept all these words, pondering them in her heart. [Lk. ii, 19]

43. And after the days of their purification were completed according to the Law of Moses, they took him into Jerusalem so that they might present him to the Lord. [Lk. ii, 22]

44. At the Nativity of Jesus, the Magi followed the brightness in the sky.

45. He wished to kill himself with his sword, thinking that the bound ones / prisoners had escaped. [Acts xvi, 27]

II.   1. In tempore oblātiōnis, Lēvīta dōna populī prōferet.

2. Cum Paulus ā mīlitibus vīnctus est, ante rēgem loquī cōactus est.

3. Ut pūrgātiōnem populī sīgnificet, sacerdōs (eōs) aquā sparget.

4. Ad Jēsūm īnfirmī lātī sunt ut sānārentur.

5. Nocte dīves ad Jēsūm vēnit ut eum rogāret dē rēgnō caelī.

Readings

1.   Asperges Me (Ps. li, 7, 1)

You will sprinkle me, Lord, with hyssop, and I will be cleansed: you will wash me, and I will be made white above the snow. Have pity on me, God, according to your great mercy. Glory (be) to the Father, and to the Son, and to the Holy Spirit. As it was in the beginning, and (is) now, and (will be) always, and forever and ever. Amen.

2.   Salutis Humanae, by St. Ambrose (340–397).

Sower of human salvation,
Jesus, delight of hearts,
founder of a redeemed world,
and chaste light of lovers:

By what clemency were you conquered,
so that you might bear our sins?
So that, (though) innocent, you might submit to death,
in order to take us away from death?

You burst through the lower world:
you take away the chains from those who are bound;
victor in a noble triumph
you sit at the right hand of (your) father.

May forgiveness compel you
to make good our losses,
and may you enrich with (your) blessed light
(those who are) possessed of your countenance.
You, leader and pathway to the stars,
may you be a turning post for our hearts,
may you be the joy of (our) tears,
may you be the sweet reward of (our) life.

3.   Peter's Discourse in Caesarea (II), Acts x, 40–48.

This one did God raise on the third day and gave him to be made manifest not to all people, but to witnesses preordained by God, to us, who ate and drank with him after he rose from the dead; and he commanded us to preach to the people and to testify that he himself is the one who was ordained by God (to be) judge of the living and the dead. To this one all the prophets bear witness that all who believe in him receive forgiveness of sins through his name.

With Peter still saying these words, the Holy Spirit fell down upon all who were hearing the word. And they were amazed, those who (were) faithful from circumcision, those who had come with Peter, because the grace of the Holy Spirit was poured out even on the gentiles; for they heard them speaking in tongues and glorifying God. Then Peter answered: "Can anyone forbid water, so that these may not be baptized, who have received the Holy Spirit just as we (have)?" And he commanded them to be baptized in the name of Jesus Christ. Then they asked him to stay for some days.

Unit 34

Drills

I.   1.   Let there become light!

        2.   Matthias was made an apostle.

        3.   The man asked that he be made healthy.

        4.   With night having become / When night fell, we returned home.

        5.   If we preserve the word, we will be (made) saved.

        6.   It happened that heaven was opened.

II.   1.   Eleven of the apostles were in the upper room.

        2.   They had two loaves.

        3.   At the ninth hour he/she/it approached them.

        4.   Are ten thousand soldiers able to conquer twenty thousand?

        5.   After six days Paul went away.

Exercises

I.   1.   Or do I seek to please men? If I were still pleasing men, I would not be a servant of Christ! [Gal. i, 10]

2. Then after three years I went up to Jerusalem to see Cephas, and I stayed with him for fifteen days; but I did not see any other of the apostles except James the brother of the Lord. [Gal. i, 18–19]

3. For you were just like wandering sheep, but you have been converted now to the shepherd and the bishop of your souls. [I Pet. ii, 25]

4. And the eleven disciples went away into Galilee, to the mountain where Jesus had directed them. [Mt. xxviii, 16]

5. Simon Peter therefore went up and dragged the net onto the ground/shore, filled with one hundred fifty-three great fish. [Jn. xxi, 11]

6. But when Simon Peter saw (it), he fell down at the knees of Jesus, saying: "Depart from me, because I am a sinful man, Lord." [Lk. v, 8]

7. The heavenly choir rejoices, and angels sing to God; and openly he becomes shepherd to the shepherds, creator of all.

8. For John said to Herod: "It is not permitted for you to have the wife of your brother." [Mk. vi, 18]

9. And it was announced to him: "Your mother and your brothers stand outside wishing to see you." [Lk. viii, 20]

10. John to the seven churches which are in Asia: Grace to you and peace from him who is and who was and who is about to come, and from the seven spirits who are in sight of his throne. [Rev. i, 4]

11. Write therefore the things which you have seen and which are and which it is necessary to happen after these. [Rev. i, 19]

12. Blessed are you, Lord, God of all, because from your bounty we have received bread, which we offer to you, fruit of the land and of the work of human hands, from which the bread of life will be made for us.

13. I do always the things which are pleasing to him. [Jn. viii, 29]

14. Through the mystery of this water and wine may we be made partakers of his divinity, who deigned to become a partaker of our humanity.

15. But it is also written in your law that the testimony of two men is true. [Jn. viii, 17]

16. And a voice happened from the sky: "You are my beloved Son; in you I am pleased." [Mk. i, 11]

17. And he was in the desert forty days [, and forty nights]. [Mk. i, 13]

18. And Mary said: "Behold the handmaid of the Lord; let it be done to me according to your word." [Lk. i, 38]

19. But a certain man was there, being in his illness for thirty-eight years. [Jn. v, 5]

20. But after waiting for a long time and seeing that nothing evil happened in him, turning themselves around they said that he was a god. [Acts xxviii, 6]

21. For where two or three are gathered in my name, there I am in the midst of them. [Mt. xviii, 20]

22. And now I have told you, before it happens, so that, when it does happen, you will believe. [Jn. xiv, 29]

23. And other (seeds) fell onto good earth and gave fruit: and they rose and grew and offered thirty-for-one and sixty-for-one and a hundred-for-one. [Mk. iv, 8]

24. Was it not necessary that Christ suffer these things and enter into his glory? [Lk. xxiv, 26]

25. Then Jesus said to him: "Go, Satan! For it is written: *The Lord your God you will worship and you will serve him alone.*" [Mt. iv, 10]

26. And he said to them: "Is it permitted on the Sabbath to do good or evil? To save a life or to destroy it?" But they were silent. [Mk. iii, 4]

27. But I say to you that many from the east and the west will come and will recline with Abraham and Isaac and Jacob in the kingdom of heaven. [Mt. viii, 11]

28. Whom of the two do you wish that I release to you? [Mt. xxvii, 21]

29. And it came to pass in those days, he went out to the mountain to pray. [Lk. vi, 12]

30. For Christ did not please himself. [Rom. xv, 3]

31. When therefore the Samaritans had come to him, they asked him that he stay with them; and he stayed there for two days. [Jn. iv, 40]

32. And going out he followed (him) and did not know that what was done through the angel was true. [Acts xii, 9]

33. And it came to pass on another Sabbath that he entered the synagogue and taught. [Lk. vi, 6]

34. I saw water coming out of the temple, from the right side, alleluia: and all to whom that water came were saved, and they will say: Alleluia, alleluia.

35. For it is necessary to happen, but the end is not yet. [Mt. xxiv, 6]

36. But now there remain faith, hope, love, these three; but the greatest of these is love. [I Cor. xiii, 13]

37. It pleased us that we were left behind alone at Athens. [I Thess. iii, 1]

38. We do not know what has happened to him. [Acts vii, 40]

39. Then the just will shine like the sun in the kingdom of their Father. [Mt. xiii, 43]

40. And he said to them: "The Sabbath was made for man, not man for the Sabbath; and so the Son of man is master also of the Sabbath." [Mk. ii, 27–28]

41. But in church I wish to speak five words in my mind, so that I may instruct others, rather than ten thousand words on (my) tongue. [I Cor. xiv, 19]

42. And it was heard that he was at home. [Mk ii, 1]

43. But when it had become day, they did not recognize the land. [Acts xxvii, 39]

44. But now we know the praises of this pillar which the fire kindles, glowing to the honor of God.

45. Make it so that my heart burns in loving Christ God, so that I may be acceptable to him.

46. The side of Christ has been penetrated with the sword of a soldier.

47. Mary, having given birth to Jesus, has become the Mother of God.

48. Sinners, we ask you, hear us, that you may spare us.

49. Who do you think that (man) is, that both the wind and the sea obey him? [Mk. iv, 41]

50. They came therefore and saw where he was staying, and they stayed with him that day; the hour was about the tenth. [Jn. i, 39]

51. This is my beloved Son, in whom I am well pleased; listen to him. [Mt. xvii, 5]

52. May your souls be made chaste unto the obedience of love.

53. Do not harm those who harm you.

54. In the spirit of humility and in contrite heart may we be accepted by you, Lord; and may our sacrifice be so made in your sight today, that it may please you, Lord God.

55. You do not cease to gather your people to yourself, so that from the rising of the sun to (its) setting a pure offering may be made to your name.

56. With sincere hearts, shaped by divine instruction, let us begin the rite of Communion.

57. And received into the odor of sweetness, may it be mingled with the heavenly bodies.

58. That, I say, (is) the morning star, which does not know a setting.

59. There stood the mother grieving / tearful next to the cross.

60. Let us live in peace and sanctity.

61. Just as the rays of the sun shine upon us, so the love of God illuminates us.

62. No servant is able to serve two masters. [Lk. xvi, 13]

63. Jesus used to say that it was necessary for him to die and, on the third day, to rise.

64. And he said to him: "Take your bill and sit down quickly, (and) write fifty." [Lk. xvi, 6]

II.   1. Duodecim virī apostolī factī sunt ā Jēsū.

    2. Licet sānāre sabbatō?

    3. Sī Deō placēre volumus, necesse est nōs mandātīs ejus oboedīre.

    4. Procidēns vir rogāvit Jēsūm ut eī parcat.

    5. Trēs diāconī ōrāvērunt ut fierī sacerdōtēs dīgnārentur.

Readings

1.   The Conversion of Saul (I), Acts ix, 1–12.

But Saul, still breathing threats and murder against the disciples of the Lord, went to the chief priest and asked him for letters to the synagogues at Damascus, so that if he found any of this way, men or women, he might lead them bound into Jerusalem. And when he was making the journey, it happened that he was approaching Damascus, and suddenly a light from heaven shone around him, and falling onto the ground he heard a voice saying to him: "Saul, Saul, why do you persecute me?" And he said, "Who are you, Lord?" And he (said): "I am Jesus, whom you persecute! But rise and go into the city, and it will be told to you what you must do." But those men who were traveling with him stood, astounded, hearing indeed a voice, but seeing no one. And Saul rose from the ground and with his eyes opened was seeing nothing; and drawing him by the hand they led him into Damascus. And for three days he was not seeing and did not eat or drink.

But there was a certain disciple in Damascus, by name Ananias, and the Lord said to him in a vision: "Ananias!" But he said: "Behold, (it is) I, Lord!" And the Lord (said) to him: "Rising, go into the street which is called Straight, and seek in the house of Judas (a man) of Tarsus, Saul by name; for behold, he is praying and he has seen a man by name Ananias going in and placing (his) hands on him, so that he may take back (his) vision.

2.   Christum Ducem, by St. Bonaventure (1221–1274).

Let our joyful assembly praise Christ (our) leader, who through the cross has rescued us from (our) enemies; let heaven rejoice with praises.

Let the strong pain of your death and the outpouring of (your) blood afflict (our) hearts, so that we may seek you, Jesus, our deliverance.

Through the blessed scars, let the spittle, the scourges, the lashes be granted (as) eternal gifts of Christ, pleasing to us.

Let the blood of your wounds, in which we have all been washed, touch our heart, so that it may mourn (you), nourishing founder of the stars.

Imbue us, Savior, with the gifts of your Passion, by which you wish faithfully to give us blessed joys.

Unit 35

Drills

I. 1. The apostles were praying in the upper room.

2. Jesus was praying on the mountain.

3. For three days he was not seeing / could not see.

4. We will be singing in the church.

5. They are sitting in silence.

II. 1a. audīsse: perfect active infinitive ("to have heard")
1b. audīvisse

2a. dēlērunt: 3rd pl. perfect active indicative ("they [have] destroyed")
2b. dēlēvērunt

3a. amāstis: 2nd pl. perfect active indicative ("you [have] loved")
3b. amāvistis

4a. cūrāssent: 3rd pl. pluperfect active subjunctive ("they might have healed")
4b. cūrāvissent

5a. laudārim: 1st sg. perfect active subjunctive ("I may have praised")
5b. laudāverim

6a. abiērunt: 3rd pl. perfect active indicative ("they have gone away /
    went away")
6b. abīvērunt

7a. fīniit: 3rd sg. perfect active indicative ("he/she/it [has] ended")
7b. fīnīvit

8a. nescierat: 3rd sg. pluperfect active indicative ("he/she/it had not
    known")
8b. nescīverat

9a. exiimus: 1st pl. perfect active indicative ("we have gone out /
    went out")
9b. exīvimus

Exercises

I.   1. Then Herod, with the Magi secretly summoned, diligently
        learned from them the time of the star which appeared to them,
        and sending them into Bethlehem he said: "Go and inquire dili-
        gently about the boy; and when you find out, report to me, so
        that I, coming, may worship him." [Mt. ii, 7–8]

     2. Then all those virgins rose and trimmed their lamps. [Mt. xxv, 7]

     3. Behold, I am living forever. [Rev. i, 18]

     4. And on the next day, when they left Bethany, he was hungry.
        [Mk. xi, 12]

     5. And Jesus said to Simon: "Do not be afraid; from this (time) now
        you will be catching men." [Lk. v, 10]

     6. For I was hungry, and you gave to me to eat. [Mt. xxv, 35]

     7. And again he began to teach beside the sea. [Mk. iv, 1]

     8. Hail, our King, Son of David, Redeemer of the world, whom the
        prophets predicted would come as Savior to the house of Israel.

     9. Save your people, Lord, and bless your inheritance, and rule over
        them and lift them up forever.

    10. It pleased God . . . that he should reveal his Son to me. [Gal. i,
        15–16]

11. Come, let us slay him, and we will have his inheritance. [Mt. xxi, 38]

12. The world cannot hate you, but it hates me, because I produce testimony about it, that its works are evil. [Jn. vii, 7]

13. But he, with them all having been ejected, took the father of the girl and the mother and those who were with him, and went in where the girl was [lying down]. [Mk. v, 40]

14. But Herod, when he saw Jesus, was very glad: for he was desiring for a long time to see him, because he was hearing about him, and he was hoping to see some sign made by him. [Lk. xxiii, 8]

15. It is necessary therefore that (one) of these men—who had assembled with us in all the time in which the Lord Jesus went in and went out among us, beginning from the baptism of John until the day on which he was taken up from us—that one of these (men) become with us a witness of his resurrection. [Acts i, 21–22]

16. Let mother Church also rejoice, adorned with the rays of so great a light.

17. Let the earth too rejoice, illumined with such great rays: and enlightened with the splendor of the eternal King, let (the earth) perceive that it has sent away the gloom of the whole world.

18. O truly blessed night, which despoiled the Egyptians and enriched the Hebrews!

19. Grant the tranquility of perpetual peace!

20. Let the morning star find its flames!

21. O wonderful graciousness of your goodness around us!

22. He puts to flight hatreds, prepares peace, and humbles empires.

23. It anyone says: "I love God," and hates his brother, he is a liar. [I Jn. iv, 20]

24. And behold: you will be silent and you will not be able to speak until the day on which these things happen. [Lk. i, 20]

25. Then Paul, with his hand outstretched, began to render his account. [Acts xxvi, 1]

26. And he came preaching in their synagogues through all Galilee and casting out demons. [Mk. i, 39]

27. Then Jesus began to explain to his disciples that it was necessary for him to go to Jerusalem and to suffer many things from the elders and the chief priests and the scribes and to be killed and to rise on the third day. [Mt. xvi, 21]

28. With gladness he rejoices because of the voice of the bridegroom. [Jn. iii, 29]

29. John the Baptist was in the desert preaching the baptism of repentance for the forgiveness of sins. [Mk. i, 4]

30. Be kind, spare us, Lord!

31. But the woman, fearing and trembling, knowing what had been done to her, came and fell down before him and told him all the truth. [Mk. v, 33]

32. When Jesus saw him lying down and knew that he had (been there) for a long time now, he said to him: "Do you wish to be healed?" [Jn. v, 6]

33. And they were filled with fear, saying: "We have seen wondrous things today." [Lk. v, 26]

34. But a certain (man) said to him from the crowd: "Teacher, tell my brother to divide (his) inheritance with me." [Lk. xii, 13]

35. Jesus said to them: "I am the bread of life. He who comes to me will not be hungry." [Jn. vi, 35]

36. And going out they preached that they do penance; and they cast out many demons. [Mk. vi, 12–13]

37. And indeed, although he was the Son, he learned obedience from these things which he suffered. [Heb. v, 8]

38. And he said to them: "With eagerness have I desired to eat this Paschal meal with you, before I suffer. For I say to you: I will not eat it until it is fulfilled in the kingdom of God." [Lk. xxii, 15–16]

39. By commanding, did we not command you not to teach in this name? And behold, you have filled Jerusalem with your teaching and you wish to bring upon us the blood of this man. [Acts v, 28]

40. Therefore, you, my son, be strong in the grace which is in Christ Jesus, and what you have heard from me through many witnesses, these things entrust to faithful men, who will be fit also to teach others. [II Tim. ii, 1–2]

II.   1.   Jēsūs multa discipulīs revēlāns erat dē ruīnā Jerūsalem.

   2.   Firmāmur ope Deī.

   3.   Turba coepit ēsurīre.

   4.   Mulierēs magnō timōre timēbant dōnec angelus eās allocūtus est.

   5.   Et Jēsūs dīxit eīs sedēre ut mandūcārent.

   6.   Apostolī Galilaeā circumientēs erant, et evangelizantēs et spīritūs malōs ējicientēs.

[Note: Alternatively, the imperfect indicative may be used in #1 and #6 instead of the Greek periphrastic discussed in Unit 35: **revēlābat, circumibant, evangelizābant, ējiciēbant**.]

Readings

1.   The Conversion of Saul (II), Acts ix, 13–22.

   But Ananias answered: "Lord, I have heard from many about this man, how much evil he has done to your saints in Jerusalem; and from the chief priests he has the authority to arrest all who call on your name." But the Lord said to him: "Go, because that (man) is my vessel of choice to carry my name before Gentiles and kings and the sons of Israel; for I will show him how much it is necessary that he suffer on behalf of my name." And Ananias went away and entered the house and, placing his hands on (him), said: "Brother Saul, the Lord—Jesus who appeared to you on the road on which you were coming—has sent me, so that you may see and be filled with the Holy Spirit." And immediately scales, as it were, fell from his eyes, and he received (his) sight. And rising he was baptized and, when he had taken food, he grew strong.

And for some days he was with the disciples who were in Damascus and at once in the synagogues he proclaimed Jesus, that this one is the Son of God. But all who heard were stunned and were saying: "Is not this (man) the one who was attacking those in Jerusalem who invoked that name, and he had come here to this (place) to lead them, bound, to the chief priests?" But Saul was becoming stronger and was confounding the Jews who lived in Damascus, affirming that this one is the Christ.

2.   The Lord's Prayer.

(a) Mt. vi, 9–13.

Thus therefore will you pray:
Our Father, you who are in heaven,
may your name be sanctified,
may your kingdom come,
may your will be done
just as (it is done) in heaven and on earth.
Give us today our life-sustaining bread;
and forgive us our debts,
just as we too forgive our debtors;
and may you not lead us into temptation,
but free us from Evil.

(b) Lk. xi, 2–4.

And he said to them: "When you pray, say:
Father,
may your name be sanctified,
may your kingdom come;
give us daily our daily bread,
and forgive us our sins,
for indeed we ourselves too forgive everyone who owes us,
and may you not lead us into temptation."